T0346427

GEORGETOWN'S SECOND FOUNDER

STATI UNITI

di Arrowsmith.

Milano da Pietro e Giuseppe Vallardi.

Longitudine Ovest del Meridiano di Parigi.

Deposto alla I C Biblioteco

Georgetown's Second Founder

Fr. Giovanni Grassi's
*News on the Present Condition
of the Republic of the United States
of North America*

Translated and Introduced
by Roberto Severino

WASHINGTON, DC / GEORGETOWN UNIVERSITY PRESS

The publisher is not responsible for third-party websites or their content. URL links were active at time of publication.

Library of Congress Cataloging-in-Publication Data

Names: Grassi, Giovanni, 1775–1849, author. | Severino, Roberto, translator.
Title: Georgetown's Second Founder : Fr. Giovanni Grassi's News on the Present Condition of the Republic of the United States of North America / Roberto Severino, Translator.
Other titles: Notizie sullo stato presente della repubblica degli Stati Uniti dell'America Settentrionale, scritte al principio del 1822. English | Fr. Giovanni Grassi's News on the present condition of the Republic of the United States of North America
Description: Washington, DC : Georgetown University Press, 2021. | Includes bibliographical references and index.
Identifiers: LCCN 2020008157 | ISBN 9781647120436 (hardcover) | ISBN 9781647120443 (ebook)
Subjects: LCSH: Grassi, Giovanni, 1775–1849—Travel—United States. | United States—Description and travel. | United States—Religion.
Classification: LCC E165 .G7613 2021 | DDC 973.5/4—dc22
LC record available at https://lccn.loc.gov/2020008157

♾ This book is printed on acid-free paper meeting the requirements of the American National Standard for Permanence in Paper for Printed Library Materials.

22 21   9 8 7 6 5 4 3 2 First printing

Printed in the United States of America.

Cover design by Erin Kirk

Text design by Classic City Composition

The folio features an undated Italian version of a map of the United States by the eminent geographer and cartographer Aaron Arrowsmith. Sold in Milan by the Giuseppe and Pietro Vallardi's firm, ca. 1812–15.

Tempo verrà, che fien d'Ercole i segni
Favola vile a naviganti industri,
E i mar riposti, or senza nome, e i regni
Ignoti ancor tra voi seranno illustri.

GERUSAL. LIB., canto XV st. 30

———➤◦◄———

The time shall come that sailors shall disdain
To talk or argue of Alcides' streat,
And lands and seas that nameless yet remain,
Shall well be known, their boundaries, site and seat . . .

FROM Torquato Tasso's (1544–1595) *"Gerusalemme Liberata"* (Jerusalem Delivered),
Canto XV, first four verses of stanza 30, rendered in English in 1600 by
Edward Fairfax (1560–1635). Alcides' Streat refers to the Pillars of Hercules, the two
promontories flanking the Strait of Gibraltar.

CONTENTS

Italian map of the United States, ca. 1812–15   frontispiece

Foreword, Robert Emmett Curran   ix

Introduction: Father Giovanni Grassi, SJ, "Second Founder"
of Georgetown University   xv

Acknowledgments   xxxiii

Notizie

1   News on the Present Condition of the Republic of the
    United States of Northern America   1

2   On the Various Sects That Exist in the United States   33

3   On the Present Condition of the Catholic Religion
    in the United States   59

A Contemporary *Unicum*: The *North American Review*
Piece of 1823   79

Bibliography   95

Table of All the Most Remarkable Things to Be Found
within the Geography of the United States in North America   97

Index   101

FOREWORD

I N THE SHAPING of the Catholic Church in the early American republic, immigrant clergy and religious played a disproportionately huge role. Perhaps never have so few had such influence in developing the institutional matrix and culture of the American Catholic community, from Boston to New Orleans, and from Baltimore to Saint Louis. Most were French émigrés, such as Ambrose Maréchal, Jean Lefebvre de Cheverus, Benedict Joseph Flaget, John Dubois, Philippine Duchesne, and Louis William Dubourg. But other Europeans left their lasting imprint as well, notably John England of Ireland and Joseph Rosati of Italy. Another Italian, Giovanni Grassi, unlike the others, spent barely seven years in the United States. In that brief period, nonetheless, Grassi left his permanent mark on the first Catholic college in the United States by saving it as an educational institution and by establishing important relations between the college and the federal government. Despite his short sojourn here, he was a keen observer of the culture and economy of the young republic in the third decade of its history, as he well demonstrated in *Notizie varie sullo stato presente della repubblica degli Stati Uniti dell'America settentrionale scritte al principio del 1818* (1819). Grassi, in fact, was the only one of this distinguished immigrant cohort to publish his impressions of this country, which makes *Notizie* all the more special.

A native of Bergamo in northern Italy, Grassi had entered the Society of Jesus in 1799, when the order was still under papal suppression, except for the Byelorussian territories of eastern Poland and Lithuania, which were under the control of Catherine of Russia. The Russian ruler, valuing the Jesuit schools within her jurisdiction, had refused to allow the promulgation of the brief of suppression. Grassi's Jesuit superiors, recognizing his extraordinary intellectual and administrative talents, had expedited his training and, after his ordination in 1805, appointed him rector of a college in Russian Poland. Scarcely had he begun his tenure when he was named to a three-man mission to China. For five years he made various attempts to find a port from which to make his passage to Asia—all in vain. In the meantime, at the Jesuit college in Stonyhurst, England, he pursued studies in mathematics and astronomy. Finally, in 1810, the Jesuit superior general changed Grassi's mission from China to the United States, where some ex-Jesuits had recently rejoined the Society that survived in Russia.

Less than a year after he arrived at Georgetown College, Grassi was given a dual appointment: rector of the college and superior of the Maryland Mission. He found the college to be in a "miserable state," with crushing debts and few students ("blackguards," Grassi deemed them). Georgetown, he wrote an English Jesuit in 1811, was unlike any Jesuit college he had ever known, and he hoped never to know another such one.[1] Whereas Georgetown had, until recently, attracted students from all parts of the country as well as from Central America, now the college was losing them to colleges in Baltimore and New York, operated by Sulpicians and Jesuits, respectively.

Of immediate concern to Grassi was his legal authority as rector and superior. Legally, the college belonged to the Corporation of the Roman Catholic Clergymen of Maryland, an autonomous, self-perpetuating body, created in 1792 to protect the lands previously owned by members of the Society of Jesus before its suppression. The trustees of the corporation appointed the directors of the college, who elected its rector. Grassi effectively had to use all his considerable diplomatic and administrative skills to govern the college within this Byzantine organization, largely by coaxing the directors and trustees to go along with his plans for the college and mission. First was his audacious proposal to virtually halve the cost of boarding at Georgetown, from $220 to $125, to increase enrollment. Similar adjustments were made for commuting students. But financial adjustments alone could not save Georgetown. The faculty was barely a faculty at all, with but one priest (besides Grassi) and three scholastics (seminarians). If Georgetown was to be a college in more than designation, it needed more professors to offer a full curriculum ranging from the classics to philosophy. A consolidation of the Jesuit educational institutions in Washington and New York was the only solution to their manpower shortage. So in 1813, Grassi, with Archbishop John Carroll's backing, recalled the Jesuits teaching in New York, which drew vehement protests that they were abandoning a school in what was becoming the most important city in the country, making it "fifty times more valuable than Georgetown." Grassi, focusing on the present crisis rather than any future promise, persisted.

With a major competitor eliminated and financial restructuring in place, within a year Georgetown's student body began to be much more diverse in economic status, geographic origins, and the religious affiliations of its students as well as the occupations of their fathers. Grassi was resurrecting John Carroll's aspiration for Georgetown to be an institution "calculated for every Class of Citizens" as well as for "students of every religious profession."[2] Despite the increase in Protestant students (which by 1814 made up a quarter of the student body), the five Grassi years proved to be a golden age for vocations to the priesthood, with twenty-six students moving from Georgetown to the seminary. Georgetown, under Grassi, had become the major domestic producer of clergy for Carroll's Church.

Grassi also made the college an integral part of the intellectual and social life of Washington society. Long after his departure from Georgetown, his telescope continued to attract people to campus for observation of the heavens. He became a regular consultant to the Patent Office and the US Navy. Through regular visits to Congress and invitations to government officials, he developed valuable ties, which both promoted the college and enhanced its image in the community. He revived the public "exhibitions," which served as commencement exercises to conclude the academic year. One such exhibition included a model of the solar system, constructed under his direction, which attracted a large crowd, including US senators and representatives. In 1816 he and the college's mathematics professor launched a balloon on the college grounds as a scientific experiment.

When Grassi became the rector of Georgetown College, the institution still lacked a charter. This lack was due to no oversight. Its founder, John Carroll, wary of the intrusive tendencies of state governments toward educational institutions at the time, had deliberately avoided securing a charter that would have given the state of Maryland the legal grounds for exercising control over his newborn academy. By 1814 judicial developments had clearly established chartered colleges as private enterprises, which were protected from the overreach of government. No longer were there grounds for fearing a violation of the separation of church and state, even if the federal government was the chartering authority. Grassi knew enough of these developments to feel confident that a charter no longer was a threat to a college's independence. In the White House was a president, James Monroe, who was known to be a promoter of the civil rights of religious minorities, including Catholics. And, most serendipitous, in Congress, as a representative from North Carolina, was Georgetown's very first student and a very loyal alumnus, William Gaston, who had become a close friend of Grassi. Through Gaston, Grassi made his petition to Congress for a charter in January 1815. James Madison signed it into law in March.

Two years later, Grassi awarded Georgetown's first two degrees. By then he had assembled the most promising faculty Georgetown College had ever known, including James Wallace, who had already gained a reputation in the field of astronomy by publishing one of its first textbooks. In 1815 Congress had invited Wallace and Grassi to undertake, through astronomical observations, the calculation of the longitude of the city of Washington. This was to be the initial stage of Georgetown College's becoming the site of a national observatory. Grassi and Wallace preferred to delay the project until they had secured more precise instruments from Europe. But before that could happen, Grassi, in the early summer of 1817, reluctantly left for Europe, to serve as an agent for Leonard Neale, the Jesuit archbishop of Baltimore, who needed Rome's support in his fights with dissident clergy and lay trustees in his archdiocese. Grassi also hoped to use the trip to plead in person his own case with Jesuit superiors for more men for America as well as to raise funds for the mission.

The trip proved to be Grassi's permanent leave-taking of America. Doctors in Rome warned him that his inoperable hernia made another transatlantic crossing a very dangerous undertaking. In his stead, Grassi was reduced to sending back books for the faculty and art for a gallery he was planning to open at the college. Also, thanks to the persistence of Italian friends, he put together his impressions of the country at whose center he had been a prominent resident.

"In this work," Grassi wrote in his introduction to *Notizie*, "I have sought to describe that which most attracted my attention there and which, I hope, most deserves the attention of others." Given the briefness of the volume, it is remarkable how much of America Grassi captured in his *Notizie*. It is Jefferson's *Notes on the State of Virginia* on a national scale: a mammoth inventory of things American. Besides providing a survey of the Catholic Church in America, *Notizie* examined the diversity and extremes of its climate; the prevalence and peculiarity of its diseases and fevers; its migration patterns; the promise of its agricultural produce to create an abundance capable of eliminating hunger; its universal, flexible, complex commerce; Americans' lack of rootedness; their fast-growing manufacturing; the impact of the War of 1812 on the nascent banking industry; the inability of laws to change mores; the dispersed population's unprecedented growth; the fundamental contradiction between slavery and America's core value of freedom; the limited prospects for success in America; the reason for creating a capital independent of the states, and the prospects for its growth; the unique housing patterns in America; the architecture of public life; the inchoateness of the public character; the incipient transportation revolution; America's moral and social deficits; the importance given to education and the extraordinary literacy of Americans; the regional differences among the medical profession; the surprising state of the fine arts and the remarkably high level of the sciences in American culture; the technological development created by labor scarcity; the structure of its republican government and the abuses of its politics; the tempering of inequality by the wide availability of land; religious liberty and the less-than-strict separation of church and state in a land so awash in sects; the persistent anti-Catholicism; and the radical instability of religious affiliation.

The *Notizie* were a fitting cap to Grassi's American mission. His incisively positive evaluation of American society complemented his laying of the intellectual, religious, and legal foundations of what would eventually become one of the premier universities in the United States. Archbishop Carroll reflected in 1815 that Grassi was adding "celebrity and reputation to the character" to Georgetown College.[3] If Carroll had lived longer, in the light of Grassi's publication, he might well have revised his estimate of Italian immigrants' impact from a broader perspective. For Grassi's tenure as Georgetown rector as well as his publication on the state of his adopted country reveal his deep faith in the congruence of the Catholic religion with the American republic. By word and deed Giovanni Grassi was perhaps John Carroll's most effective disciple in advancing Carroll's republican vision for the Catholic Church in America.

Thanks to Roberto Severino's highly readable translation, this remarkable document is at last available to the American public. It provides the opportunity for those interested in the history of the early republic to appreciate the appraisal of American society that a wise Catholic newcomer was able to offer. With this publication, we are indebted to both Professor Severino and Father Grassi.

— Robert Emmett Curran

Notes

1. Grassi to William Strickland, Georgetown, October, 8, 1811, Maryland Province Archives, 453, Georgetown University Special Collections.

2. "Proposal for Establishing an Academy," in *Bicentennial History*, ed. Curran, 27.

3. Carroll to Charles Plowden, Baltimore, October 13, 1815, in Hanley, *John Carroll Papers*, 3:368.

INTRODUCTION:
FATHER GIOVANNI GRASSI, SJ,
"SECOND FOUNDER" OF
GEORGETOWN UNIVERSITY

A LTHOUGH MANY studies have dealt with the great influence that Italians have had on the United States' educational system, relatively little attention has been given, so far, to the pivotal role that Italian educators and priests have played in the making of one of the finest private institutions of higher learning of this country, Georgetown University.[1] Many of these distinguished educators and men of learning, among whom Father Angelo Secchi, SJ; Father Benedetto Sestini, SJ; and Father Giovanni Battista Pianciani, SJ, were driven from Rome to Georgetown College by the revolutionary events of 1848–49. Others, like Father Giuseppe Maria Finotti, SJ, had come but a few years earlier to serve as teacher and librarian at the fledgling institution.[2] One man, however, Father Giovanni Antonio Grassi, was destined to leave an indelible mark on the future development and fortunes of the university and to stay at its helm during the most trying period of its existence. He had come much earlier, in 1810, as the result of a series of fortuitous but challenging circumstances. It was largely through his efforts as a teacher, vice president, and president of the then–Georgetown College (1810–17) that this institution was able to survive one of the bleakest moments of its existence and, indeed, escape being extinguished altogether. Thus, he fully deserves to be called a "co-founder" or the attribute often assigned to him of "second founder" of Georgetown University.[3]

After Clement XIV's suppression of the Jesuit order with the promulgation, in 1773, of the brief *Dominus ac Redemptor*, some Jesuits were allowed to come to the United States as missionaries. Not until 1805, however, were the remaining members of the order in America notified of the verbal permission (*vivae vocis oraculum*) to reaffiliate with the small group

xv

of Jesuits from White Russia, where the brief had never been promulgated and who had officially been granted permission to continue in existence just a few years earlier. Thus, although this first of the many Catholic colleges and universities to be established in the United States was founded by John Carroll in 1789—as the "Academy at George Town, Patowmack River, Maryland," with its first student, William Gaston of North Carolina, admitted in 1791—it can be said that technically it was not founded by the Jesuits because their order had been disbanded some sixteen years earlier; nevertheless, it was created by men trained in the Society and thus, from the beginning, it must fully be considered a Jesuit institution. The circuitous ways through which the life of the promising Father John Anthony Grassi finally became indissolubly intertwined with the fate of Georgetown in themselves make a most interesting story that begs to be retold. Grassi was born in Schilpario, Bergamo, then part of the Venetian Republic, in 1775, and in 1799 he entered the Society of Jesus at Colorno, near Parma, Emilia e Romagna—the first novitiate to open after the 1773 suppression—and studied under Father Giuseppe Maria Pignatelli, "the restorer of the Society," who was canonized in 1954.[4] Still a novice in 1801, Grassi was then sent to Russia, where he completed his studies, was ordained to the priesthood, and named, in 1804, Rector of the College of Nobles attached to the College of Polotsk, Belarus.

After Pius VII's brief *Catholicae fidei* of March 7, 1801, which allowed the reestablishment of the Society only within the boundaries of Russia (*intra limites Rossiaci imperii tantum*) in 1804, there came a request from an aging French ex-Jesuit, Father Louis Poirot, who was living at the court of the Chinese emperor as a musician, to send to China some younger Jesuits to continue his apostolate there. With the endorsement of the pope, and the interest of the Russian government, which had been planning a diplomatic mission to China, the then–general of the order, Father Gabriel Gruber, acceded to the request and advised the Jesuits Father Grassi and Father Korsack, a Russian, as well as a German lay brother, to prepare for the trip. Due to the restrictive policies of the Chinese with regard to Christian missionaries, they were instructed, however, not to join a Russian diplomatic expedition that had planned to take an overland route, but to go instead to London, where it was presumed they could find a direct sea passage to Canton.

After traveling to Saint Petersburg to meet with Father General Gruber and to receive supplies and instructions, they left in three sleighs, accompanied by a Swedish interpreter, on February 2, 1805. Conquering increasing difficulties, they were able to cross into Sweden from Finland, reaching Stockholm on March 22. There, they were advised by the Russian minister in Stockholm not to trust the English promise of a passage but, instead, to try to secure passage on a ship bound for Canton in Copenhagen. In Copenhagen, however, they were unable to find a ship that would take them to China. Resuming their old plan of finding passage from England, they left for London, where, after many vicissitudes due to the inclement weather, they finally arrived on May 25. Unable to convince the director of the India Company to allow them on one of the company's ships, Father Grassi and his two companions were instructed by Father Lustyg, who had since succeeded the deceased Father Gruber as general of the order, to try to find passage on a Portuguese ship.

Accordingly, on July 29 they embarked from London on a Portuguese vessel that would ultimately take them to Lisbon. However, because, of the captain's decision to stop in Ireland to pick up more passengers and cargo, and because of ensuing unfavorable weather conditions, they were delayed in Cork until September 20, finally reaching Lisbon only on September 28.

Their stay in Portugal—a country where the decree of suppression had been severely applied, and due to alarming news of the persecution of Christians in China—lasted for over two long and frustrating years, but at least it allowed the two Jesuits to devote themselves to the study of science and, particularly, of calculus and astronomy. Lacking, however, the express approval of the pope, which could remove any obstacle to their departure as Jesuit missionaries, and with the open opposition of the Propaganda Fide, the two fathers were finally informed, on September 5, 1807, that permission had been granted to go to China provided that, like all other missionaries of the Propaganda Fide, they would submit to the jurisdiction of the vicars apostolic. They immediately informed the father general of this unwelcome development and, as expected, the condition was found unacceptable. Because of this, and also because of the impending French invasion, the two were then instructed to leave Portugal and to travel to England on a convoy of ships carrying English nationals to their motherland. They were to seek refuge at Stonyhurst College, where they could safely await further developments.

At Stonyhurst, where they arrived on December 21, 1807, Father Korsack was given the chair of moral theology and, later, entrusted with the cabinet of physics and with a class of metaphysics, while Father Grassi began teaching Italian and Latin. Urged, however, by the father general, who was still hoping to send them to China, to further their knowledge of astronomy, chemistry, and the mathematical sciences, they moved to London at the beginning of 1810. In April of that year, they received two letters: the first one ordering them to go back to Russia in order to attempt to enter China over land, and the second one telling them to postpone their departure because it had been proposed, instead, to send them to America. At the urging of the English provincial who had written to the general asking that the two be allowed to join the faculty of Stonyhurst, only Father Korsack was permitted to remain, while Father Grassi was instructed to go to America, to Georgetown College. Having left from Liverpool on August 31, 1810, Father Grassi arrived in Baltimore on October 21; and after a brief stay there, he reached his post on October 26 of that same year.[5]

In this essay I have selected for inclusion a few interesting entries from Father Grassi's hitherto unpublished diary, which was written in Italian but also includes a few words of English. Although sketchy and, at times, intentionally reserved, the diary provides us with poignant and telling glimpses of Father Grassi's sojourn in the new country—whose citizen he would later become—and of the momentous historical events he witnessed firsthand. Yet, despite the cryptic and laconic nature of these notations, from them there clearly emerges the strong and perceptive personality of a man who was very aware of the difficult task that had fallen upon him. Indeed, the factually rich details present us with a picture of a priest and educator who, though still attending to his pastoral duties, was intensely preoccupied with the uncertain fate of the young college and of its students.

Having arrived in Baltimore on October 21, fifty-two days later after leaving England's shores, and after having somewhat restored himself at the Globe Tavern from the long and perilous voyage, Grassi's first task was that of presenting himself to the Church's highest representatives in this country, Baltimore's Archbishop Carroll and the bishop-elect of Philadelphia, Father Egan. In his diary he writes, "Oct. 22, 1810: Today I had lunch with the Archbishop and dinner with the Bishop of Philadelphia; Oct. 26, 1810: After eight hours of stage coach, I arrived in Washington: an embryo of a town rather than a true town." At Georgetown he was warmly welcomed by Bishop Leonard Neale, SJ, and the community, and almost immediately was assigned the combined tasks of dean and vice president of the school.

At the time of Father Grassi's arrival, the college's situation was rather dismal. The years immediately preceding, especially the period 1806-9, must have been particularly disappointing, as even Bishop Carroll, the college founder, had grown rather pessimistic about its chances of survival and had often contemplated its closing. Father Grassi himself realized immediately that the college was in a very precarious state and that much rebuilding needed to be done, inasmuch as "there were but ten boarders and prospects for any improvements were very small." Bishop Carroll felt that the institution had sunk "to the lowest degree of discredit." In a letter dated October 8, 1811, just before being appointed as its ninth president, an obviously discouraged Father Grassi wrote of having been placed in a "melancholy situation, compelled to be a sorrowful spectator to the miserable state of this college."[6]

A sampling of typically short, yet informative, diary entries from his first years at Georgetown gives a clearer picture of what the man's thoughts and concerns must have been, and of the things and events that caught his attention and that he deemed noteworthy: "I went to the Senate House to register my name in order to obtain the American citizenship"; "I went to the Capitol to see Mr. Franzoni and Mr. Andrei, *artisti fiorentini*";[7] "I went to the Navy Yard and to the [US] President's house"; "Classes begin. 36 students and three classes formed"; "Students are awakened at 5:30 a.m.";[8] "I received a letter from Father Strickland, dated February 12."

Although, in his diary, Father Grassi does not mention the content of Father Strickland's letter, from the minutes of the Board of Directors, August 11, 1812, we learn that this letter contained the news that the general of the Society in Russia had named Father Grassi, then aged thirty-seven years, rector of Georgetown and provincial of the Jesuit Province of North America. Archbishop Carroll, however, in a letter to Father Grassi written on July 9, 1812, informed him that he could not approve the latter office "until the Society would be restored fully throughout the world." How perturbed, if at all, Father Grassi was by these turns of events we cannot really judge, as his entries continued to show the same matter-of-fact tone. From various other diary entries, we learn that in addition to his administrative duties, he also busied himself with parish duties: "April 23, 1812: Mr. (Henry) Lee gave me two pictures, a gift of Mrs. Custis (the niece [*sic*] of General Washington) for the church of Alexandria"; "Baptized two *negretti* (young Negroes); gave absolution to another;" "baptized a *negrino* (a very young Negro)"; and so on although, inevitably, the task of running the young and struggling college gradually took most of his time. "May 14, 1812: Went to the Navy Yard and saw some Italians."

At the beginning of the nineteenth century, there must have been a number of Italians, both clerics and laymen, living in Washington and in its surrounding areas, as Italian surnames, especially northern ones, appear frequently in Father Grassi's diary. Some of them, often entrepreneurs who had come to the new country to seize the business opportunities it presented, stopped at the college to see their fellow Italian and, possibly, to seek his advice. Among the names he records are a Mr. Vanini, from Florence, who came with a proposal for a lottery for the government; Mr. Scotti, a Milanese, who is a hairdresser; the two Tuscan artists Franzoni and Andrei, whose confessions he often heard; a Mr. Sacchetti from Pontiglio, Piacenza, and a former soldier in the French Army in Russia; Mr. Pietro Arata, a businessman; a Mr. Carlo Sartori; a Mr. Salomoni; and a Mr. Valaperta. On June 19, 1812, we find a dramatic entry in the diary as Father Grassi notes the publication of the declaration of war against England.

During the early war years, despite some long illness such as a bilious fever that affected him from July to October, and the constant dangers arising from the conflict, Father Grassi kept the college open and growing. On August 11 he was appointed by the Board of Directors as rector of the college; and on August 15, he also became the superior of the Maryland mission of the Society of Jesus, at that time the only Jesuit mission in North America.

Among the ensuing entries we note one, on October 14, 1812, stating that "the boys ate their '*possum*,'" obviously a fact that had aroused Father Grassi's curiosity, and another one, on March 30 of the following year, indicating that he was leaving for "Mr. Megini's springs ... to drink the sulphureous water," presumably to cure his ailments.

From his diary it appears that Father Grassi socialized often with a number of prominent citizens living in the Washington area, among whom were former governor Lee and his family, Mr. King, Mr. Gaston, the Fitzgeralds, and Eleanor "Nellie" Custis, Washington's adopted daughter, from whom, undoubtedly, he must have been kept abreast of the alarming war developments and of the other European news.

In late 1813, however, his diary records some more ordinary events, such as that on August 25, "the boys went by boat to Mount Vernon";[9] or another on October 4, according to which Father Neale, a member of the Georgetown Jesuit community, "went to perform an exorcism"; and on November 28 that he had participated in a funeral, following, in her father's coach, "the casket of Mrs. Ringgold [the daughter of Governor (Henry) Lee, who had died on November 25]."

Entries for 1814 are more momentous but are gradually growing somewhat more ominous: April 18: "Good news of a general peace in Europe"; June 5: "We went to the Navy Yard where Mr. Rose showed us how the perpetual motion worked"; June 9: "Great News! Bonaparte has been dethroned. The Pope is back in Rome. *Deo Gratias*"; July 22: "Rumors that the British troops are getting closer"; August 24: "The enemy troops enter Washington. The Navy Yard, the Capitol and the President's House are in flames. Father McElroy, an eyewitness, writes that the light coming from the East was so bright that they could read by it";[10] August 25: Father Grassi goes to Washington to inspect the damage and, while there, he meets with the deputies from Georgetown who inform him that the British have assured that the inhabitants of Georgetown will be respected provided that they remain quietly in their homes.

After the burning of the Capitol, the citizens of Georgetown and the town's mayor, without any prior consultation with Father Grassi or the Church's authorities, offered the college buildings to the Congress of the United States as a makeshift meeting place for Congress. However, out of concern for the fate of the school and its students, Father Grassi, with the support of Archbishop Carroll, strongly resisted the offer and ultimately succeeded in preserving the school's integrity and its mission.

The year 1814 came to a close with a dramatic and long-awaited development for the life of the Jesuit community. On December 9 the news arrived that Pope Pius VII had reestablished the Society of Jesus throughout the world, and on the same day a *Te Deum* and the *Veni Creator* were recited in thanksgiving.

On January 27, 1815, US Representative William Gaston, Georgetown College's first pupil, at Father Grassi's urging, presented to Congress the petition of the president and directors of the College of Georgetown that they be invested with the authority and power to grant degrees. The bill passed in the House of Representatives on February 4 and in the Senate on February 27. On March 1, the same day on which the Senate ratified the

Peace Treaty between the United States and England, President Madison signed the act granting Georgetown its charter.

Once Father Grassi had achieved recognition for the college, his new diary entries reflect events of a more normal nature, such as that of the following December 3, from which we learn that Archbishop Carroll, age eighty years, had died. Another one of the same month, on December 27, 1815, tells us that, the legal five years of probation having expired, Grassi was made a US citizen by the Washington Court.[11] Others deal more directly with the intimate nature of Georgetown College life as it was then: April 18, 1816: "The boys went on a steamboat which got stuck and remained on the river till midnight." September 15: "The boys went to the races." April 25, 1817: "Mrs. (Henry) Clay took her son away from the college lest he became a Catholic."

The college during Father Grassi's tenure must have attained a high degree of respectability and a good academic reputation as Henry Clay's son was not, by any means, the only youngster of a prominent family who attended the college during this period. A quick perusal of the *Diario* shows other such names: General Mason's nephew; Thomas Lee, the governor's nephew; William Lee, the son of the then–American consul at Bordeaux; Trevanion Dallas, the son of the secretary of the Treasury, A. James Dallas; and many others. Finally, a diary entry made on June 28, 1817, tells us that Father Grassi traveled back to Italy, arriving in Rome on September 11 of the same year.

"A superior man in mind, learning, character, administrative ability, as well as in his cultivated and refined manners," when he left for Italy on a delicate Church mission, Father Grassi must have been aware of what he had accomplished.[12] Not only had he been instrumental in promoting and keeping alive Georgetown College during very insidious and trying times, but, indeed, he had succeeded in preventing its very extinction. During his tenure there, he had shielded the college from the many external dangers caused by the War of 1812, while preventing the handing over to Congress of the school's buildings and, at the same time, securing the charter that allowed Georgetown to be the first Catholic degree-granting institution of higher learning in this country. Moreover, and perhaps more important, he had also protected the institution from the many attempts made on its integrity from within the order. Undoubtedly the most important of Father Grassi's deeds was that of resisting the repeated attempts aimed at closing down the college and converting it into a house of novitiate or transferring the school to New York.

In 1810 Father Anthony Kohlmann, a German, later oddly to become president of Georgetown College, had opened in New York, at the corner of Fifth Avenue and 50th Street, the Literary Institution, which had met with considerable success. However, since Father Kohlmann insisted on a staff of Jesuits only, the only place from where he could draw additional faculty was Georgetown College—hence, his insistence on moving the college and its faculty to New York, "a more suitable and central place." Father Grassi, however, with Archbishop Carroll's support,[13] strongly resisted this idea, and, using the very same reason of understaffing, in 1813 they "concluded to call the Fathers and Brothers from New York to Georgetown, and, of course, to close the [New York] Institution."[14] Father Kohlmann himself was later added to the Georgetown faculty and made master of novices.

Coming from Europe, Father Grassi, unlike some of his American counterparts, felt conflicted about slavery. Throughout his book he makes pointed comments on it, sometimes contrasting the reality of slavery with the ideals of the American founding and at other times demonstrating some commiseration for the enslaved individuals. For instance, in the chapter on population in America he writes,

> About one-seventh of the population consists of Negroes, who are held as slaves in open contradiction of one of the first articles of the general constitution of that republic, which declares that liberty is an inherent and inalienable right of man. I cannot deny, however, that there are some good reasons for not granting freedom all at once to the Negroes.... The importation of foreign slaves is strictly prohibited today, but, in spite of these measures, the greedy still often succeed in continuing to trade in slaves. In fact, the traffic of those poor people within the country is still permitted by civil law. Men are sold to men, and in the land of liberty one often hears the mournful sound of the rattling of slave chains. In many states of the Union, Negroes are treated well and are better nourished than European peasants, but in many others they are left in total ignorance of religion, no attention is paid to their morals, and they are neither baptized nor encouraged to unite in the sacred bonds of matrimony. The greedy master cares only that they work hard.[15]

In the chapter dedicated to literature, commenting on the great importance that gazettes had at that time in America in educating and informing the general population, he definitively nails down the previous point: "Sometimes a European can barely contain his indignation or laughter upon reading on the same page [of a gazette] an enthusiastic praise of liberty together with an announcement of a man's intention to buy or sell so many slaves; or that such a Negro is in prison because of an attempted escape from a 'hero of freedom.'"

And yet Father Grassi was also a participant in the world of Maryland slavery. Despite his strong feelings about slavery in the abstract, we know that Grassi had encounters with enslaved individuals (at the time Grassi was president of Georgetown, there were several enslaved men and women working on campus) and that these encounters produced complex and contradictory feelings in him. On one hand, Father Grassi recognized enslaved people as children of God, equally worthy of salvation. Although not an abolitionist, he commented forcefully on what the US Constitution promised, and what the states of the Union, especially those in the South, practiced.

On the other hand, Father Grassi was part of a world that saw slavery as an indispensable institution. For example, just weeks before Father Grassi returned to Italy he was involved in facilitating the transfer of eleven people bequeathed to the Maryland Jesuits by John Ashton, a former Jesuit. On February 6, 1817, he wrote a letter to Brother Joseph Marshall, overseer of the Inigoes plantation, accompanied by the handwritten list of the names of the eleven slaves, announcing their arrival. In this letter, he describes his support for enslaved people marrying, but also negotiates over the price of the wife of a man named Clem. Grassi's ability simultaneously to endorse marriage but decline to pay the sum for Clem's wife shows the complexity of his position.

Grassi also raises the issue of slavery again in the final chapter of *Notizie*, and the conclusion of this chapter gives us insight into Catholic doctrine and practice at the time:

> I must not omit the very great consolation which the Negroes bring to the missionary. Although they are poor slaves and so abject in the eyes of the world, some of them are chosen souls filled with such beautiful sentiments of true piety that they move one to tears, and the missionary himself is further encouraged to work for the glory of God. The frequent

offering of their labors to the Lord, their patient endurance of ill treatment from unprincipled masters, their obedience for the love of God,
and the recitation of the rosary when possible, are the devotions chiefly
recommended to them, and which they for the most part practice; consequently, Catholic slaves are preferred to all others, because they are more
docile and obedient to their masters.

Here we see Grassi lauding the stereotype of the obedient slave and es-
pousing Catholic doctrine that encouraged enslaved people to be obedient
to their masters. Yet, at the same time that Grassi is writing this, we know
that the Jesuits were experiencing resistance, with the enslaved suing
them for their freedom and running away. We do not know how Grassi
reconciled his beliefs and his observations or if he saw the contradictions
that we see. Still, his *Notizie* provide evidence of Catholic attitudes toward
slavery and the enslaved from a unique vantage point.

On June 28, 1817, after being asked by Bishop Neale to represent him
"on a matter vital to the Church of America, . . . the so-called Charleston
Schism," Father Grassi left for Rome, which he reached after a fifty-six-
day trip, never to return.[16] Having, in fact, accomplished his mission, he
was about to make plans to come back to his beloved America when, because of a fracture caused by a fall and a hernia, he was forbidden by his
doctor from making the long and perilous trip and was instead ordered
by the father general to remain in Italy. His superiors, however, could not
let his talents go to waste, and thus he was entrusted with other duties. In
Italy, at various times Father Grassi was appointed rector of the College
of the Nobles in Turin and confessor to the king and queen of Piedmont
and Sardinia, rector of the Propaganda College in Rome, rector of the
College of Nobles in Naples, and assistant to the general of the Society,
in the latter capacity also overseeing the matters of the Maryland
province.

In 1818, stressing at the onset that it was meant primarily for Italian
readers who knew little about contemporary America, he published in
Rome the first of three editions of his important and hitherto untranslated
"Americanum": *Notizie varie sullo stato presente della repubblica degli Stati
Uniti dell'America Settentrionale* (Various News on the Present Condition
of the Republic of the United States in North America).

The question has been raised on how Grassi's account would relate to
the work of the French patrician Alexis de Tocqueville (1805–59), who in

1831 came to America with Count Gustave de Beaumont (1802–66), a fellow lawyer related by marriage to the marquis of Lafayette, with whom he traveled widely to study the new country's penal system and the effects of democracy and republicanism. Upon returning to France, he and de Beaumont published their findings on the US penal system; and later, in 1835 and 1840, de Tocqueville published the two-volume work *Democracy in America*, in which he also warned the reader on the possible dangerous effects of too extreme freedom and individualism, while de Beaumont published *Marie: Ou l'esclavage aux États-Unis* (Marie: Or Slavery in the United States) in 1840, in which he disparaged the institution of slavery and its harmful effects on public morality. However we know that Father Grassi had already published his three editions of *Notizie* in Italy, in 1818, 1819, and 1822, and respectively in Rome, Milan, and Turin, nor do we have any reason to believe that the two Frenchmen were directly acquainted with Father Grassi's work. The only thing we can surmise is that all of them were imbued with the ideas of the Enlightenment and to a certain degree with the idealism of the French Revolution.

Although charged with many important responsibilities in many parts of Italy, Father Grassi always thought longingly of the exciting and productive years he had spent in America, and to the fledgling institution on the Potomac River he had so skillfully led and nurtured in the early and crucial years, and he frequently kept in touch with the religious brothers he had met in America. To confirm this, while recently perusing one of the copies of the 1819 second edition of *Notizie* preserved in Georgetown University's Library, much to my surprise, attached to it I was most pleased to find an original holograph letter that Father Grassi had sent from Rome on March 28, 1846, addressed to "Rev. John McElroy, at the College, United States, Maryland, Georgetown, DC."[17] In it, after sending special greetings to all his confreres at the college, and "in particular to the Italian students," he asks that to the latter the sad news be related of the passing of four Italian Jesuits they probably knew. He then informs Father McElroy of some momentous events taking place in Italy and France: the unwelcome internecine polemics initiated by "a Turin's priest (Vincenzo Gioberti), now in Bruxelles, who has published a most bitter and virulent declamation against our Society," and that Father Luigi Pellico, SJ, brother of the then–famous writer Silvio Pellico, has endeavored to answer with moderation and with the evidence of facts. He then dwells on the French Jesuits' ill treatment of their fellow Society members in France and of the conflictual presence in Rome of the French ambassador Pellegrino Rossi, who had been "sent here for the purpose of obtaining from His Holiness a total suppression of our Society in France."[18]

In all likelihood because of his American citizenship, during the 1848–49 Revolution in Rome, Father Grassi had the distinction of being the only Jesuit permitted to stay openly in the city as a guest of the famed classicist and philologist Angelo Cardinal Mai. He died in Rome on December 12, 1849, aged seventy-four, a few days after being attacked by a robber and while still living in the Cardinal's household.[19]

"Probably no other ecclesiastic of the day enjoyed in greater measure the esteem and confidence of the hierarchy."[20] After Father Grassi's departure, Georgetown College suffered twelve years of decline, and between 1817 and 1829 a succession of no less than seven presidents tried to carry on his work.[21] His legacy, however, proved to be an enduring one, and the college finally prospered again. In 1842, in his *American Notes*, Charles Dickens could observe, "At George Town, in the suburbs, there is a Jesuit college; delightfully situated, and, so far as I had the opportunity of seeing, well managed. Many persons who are not members of the Romish Church, avail themselves, I believe, of these institutions, and for the advantageous opportunities they afford.... The heights of this neighborhood, above the Potomac River, are very picturesque; and are free, I should conceive, from some of the insalubrities of Washington."[22]

Notes

1. This introduction has been adapted from an early paper of mine of almost the same title written many years ago that appeared in *Support and Struggle*, ed. Tropea, Miller, and Beattie-Repetti, 22–32. The English translation of Grassi's work has been done from the third and final revised edition of *Notizie sullo stato presente della repubblica degli Stati Uniti dell'America settentrionale* (Turin: Chirio & Mina, 1822). This later edition by Chiro & Mina was reprinted in 1823. In the 1818 first Rome edition and the subsequent 1819 Milan edition, the title was *Notizie varie sullo stato presente della repubblica degli Stati Uniti dell'America settentrionale* (*Various news . . .*), whereas in the 1822 Turin edition and its 1823 reprint, the word "*varie*" no longer appears.

2. Barringer, "They Came to Georgetown"; Daley, *Georgetown University*; Ryan, "Reminiscences."

3. Curran, *Bicentennial History*; Daley, *Georgetown University*; Ryan, "Reminiscences."

4. March, *El Restaurador de la Compañía de Jesus.*

5. The unsigned article in *Woodstock Letters* 4, no. 1 (May 1875): 136, states that Father Grassi arrived in Baltimore on October 20. However, other accounts (Garraghan, "John Anthony Grassi"), and Father Grassi himself in his *Diario*, give October 21 as the date of arrival. Only a photostat copy of the 166-page diary is to be found in the Georgetown University Library, while the original is housed in the Archives of the General of the Society of Jesus in Rome.

    6. Daley, *Georgetown University*, 164–66.

    7. Actually, Andrei and Franzoni were brought in from Carrara, Tuscany, the town that is world renowned for the marble quarries and for the skill of its marble carvers. Recognizing the lack of native stone carvers and artists needed for the US Capitol, Thomas Jefferson had written to his Italian friend Filippo Mazzei (1730–1816) seeking his help in securing some, and many arrived. The first to come were Giovanni Andrei (1770–1824) and his brother-in-law Giuseppe Franzoni (1780–1815), who arrived in 1806. The latter who would carve the great spread eagle was also entrusted by B. H. Latrobe with the sculpting of the statue of "Liberty" and the "Indian corncob" columns capitals. Among the other notable Italian artists who followed were Giuseppe's younger brother Carlo Franzoni (1788–1819), who was brought in to help in the restoration of the artwork vandalized in the British's torching of the Capitol and who is the author of the monumental allegorical marble carving representing the passage of time "Car of History" clock for the Hall of Representatives and of an allegorical plaster relief representing "Justice," the only permanent decoration in the old Supreme Court chamber; Iacopo Iardella (1793–1831), who, among other tasks given him by Latrobe, carved the "tobacco" capitals of the columns placed in the Senate's lobby; Antonio Capellano (1780–1840), who had studied under Canova, carved the bas reliefs in the Capitol Rotunda of General Washington and of Captain John Smith and Pocahontas; Enrico Causici (1790–1833), who worked at the Capitol from 1822 to 1832, and so on until the arrival, much later, of Constantino Brumidi (1805–80), who with his assistants decorated with frescoes the walls of the Capitol and conceived and almost single-handedly painted "The Apotheosis of Washington" and almost all the great "Frieze of American History" in the Capitol's Rotunda.

    8. J. T. Durkin, SJ—in his *Georgetown University: First in the Nation's Capital*, 12–13—gives this account of the daily routine then followed at Georgetown: "The boys rose in Summer at 5:00 a.m. and in Winter at 5:30.... At 5:45 came morning prayers, then Mass at 6:00. Study until 7:45, then breakfast. Classes began at 8:15 and continued until 11:15, when the students walked in silence, single file according to height, to dinner. Dinner was followed by 'recreation' or play time for an hour and half. Afternoon classes were held from 2:15 to 4:45, followed by a half hour's recreation. Another study period began at 5:30, with supper at 7:00. After night prayers, bedtime was 8:30."

    9. Mount Vernon was a popular destination for the students' outings, and on this occasion too they must have been received by Col. Washington, the General's nephew. (See Durkin, 13.)

    10. Daley, *Georgetown University*.

11. "Apparently, Fr. Grassi never renounced his American citizenship since, nine years later, a passport was issued to him by the American consul at Genoa, with the following wording: Reverend John Grassi, citizen of the United States of America, aged 49, five feet nine inches in height, chestnut colored hair and eyebrows, and remaining features of the average type." Garraghan, "John Anthony Grassi."

12. Ryan, "Reminiscences."

13. In a letter to Father Grassi, dated November 11, 1812, Archbishop Carroll had already reassured him of his support: "If either the College of Georgetown is to be discontinued or the Literary Institution near New York, undoubtedly it must be the latter" (Daley, *Georgetown University*, 174). In yet another letter to Father Charles Plowden, at Stonyhurst, dated December 12, 1813, Archbishop Carroll stood firm in his decision: "Mr. Grassi has revived the College of G. Town, which has received great improvements in the number of students and course of studies. His predecessor (Fr. Francis Neale, SJ, 1809–1812), with the same good intentions had no ability for his station, and was nominated by a strange combination.... Fr. Kohlmann, with his companions at New York, had done much for Religion, and their little College would do well, too, if it could be supplied with proper teachers. Mr. Kohlmann is unwilling to receive any but members of his body, and there are too few to supply that place and G. Town; so that if he persists in his resolution, his institution must be dissolved" *Woodstock Letters* 10, no. 2 (1881): 108–9.

14. McElroy, "Accounts of the Restoration of the Society in U.S."; see also McElroy, "Errors in His Accounts of the Restoration of the Society in the U.S."

15. Daley, *Georgetown University*, 201.

16. In addition to Giovanni Grassi in those years, there were other Italians who had written or would write about Northern America. One of the first modern Italian historians to do so, especially on the subject of America's native population, was Giovanni Rinaldo Carli (1720–95), a polymath born in Capo d'Istria, Venetian Republic, whose two-volume work *Delle lettere americane* (On American Letters) was first published in Cosmopoli (i.e., Florence) in 1780. The work is mainly a confutation of a book written a few years earlier by the Dutch-born Cornelius De Pauw (1739–99) on the origins of the American Indians titled *Recherches philosophiques sur les Américains: Ou mémoires intéressants pour servir à l'histoire de l'espèce humaine* (Philosophical Studies on the Americans: Or an Interesting Account to Be Used toward a Compilation of a History of Human Kind), which was surreptitiously first published in Berlin but then published in London in 1768. Although he never traveled to America, De Pauw depicted the Northern American Indians as inferior to Northern and Western Europeans and as being sluggish, vengeful, cruel, of weak intellect, and restrained in speaking because of their inability to formulate original ideas. In addition to Carli, many other Europeans and Americans such as Jefferson and Madison also rallied against De Pauw's opinions. Carli's major work was, however, the erudite four-volume *Antichità Italiche* (Italian Antiquities), 1788–90, in which he reconstructs a complex picture of Italian politics, culture, and the arts from before the establishment of the Roman Empire, and then during and after it, until the sixteenth century—and especially of

the Italian Peninsula, still divided into small principalities, republics, and kingdoms, whose political unity would be finally achieved only in 1861–70.

Another important Italian thinker and writer of the time was Filippo Mazzei (1730–1816), a native of Poggio a Caiano, Tuscany, whose earlier life was dedicated to medical studies. In 1755 he traveled to Smirne and Asia Minor, and in 1756 he went to London, where he began teaching Italian. In London he met Benjamin Franklin and other citizens of the North American colonies, who asked him to help introduce in America the silkworm, the olive tree, and some Italian grape varietals. Accompanied by Italian farmers in 1773, Mazzei traveled to America, where he met Thomas Jefferson, who befriended him and provided him with suitable arable land. An enlightened and staunch partisan of American independence, he wrote several articles in the *Virginia Gazette* under the nom de plume of "Furioso." In 1779 he was sent to Europe on a mission by Patrick Henry, the governor of Virginia, to negotiate a loan from the Tuscan government; but the attempt was blocked by Benjamin Franklin, who believed that loans from foreign powers could be secured only by the national government. Thus, in 1783 he returned to America. In 1785 he traveled to Paris, where he forcefully opposed the opinions of the Abbé de Mably, who had criticized the new American Constitution. While in Paris, in 1788 he published the important four-volume work *Recherches historiques et politiques sur les États-Unis de l'Amerique Septentrionale* (Historical and Political Studies on the United States in Northern America). He continued corresponding with American political leaders, and on April 24, 1796, Jefferson sent him a controversial letter, in which he criticized the Federalist leaders, and by implication George Washington, for being biased in favor of a monarchical system. Somehow the newspapers got hold of this letter, and its publication caused a serious political rift.

Finally, we must mention Carlo Botta (1766–1837), yet another prolific Italian historian, and a nationalist and republican, who was later to be honored by the French government with the Légion d'Honneur. Among Botta's many works was the seminal, well-documented account of the American War of Independence, *Storia della Guerra dell'Indipendenza degli Stati Uniti di America* (History of the War of Independence of the United States of America), which was published in Paris in 1809. In 1819 there followed a revised Italian version and, in 1820, the frequently reprinted first American edition, published in Philadelphia by Lydia R. Bailey for the translator Alexander Otis, which ranks as the first significant treatment of the American Revolution published in America. This work, mainly based on original documents and maps provided by the Marquis de Lafayette—as well as on interviews of witnesses, reports from American friends, and English accounts and diaries—extolled the purity and the idealistic intent of the American revolutionaries whose actions could be of example to Italian patriots and spur and inspire them to emulation.

17. Father John McElroy (1782–1877) was born in Ireland. He arrived in the United States in 1803, in 1806 enrolled at Georgetown College, and in 1817 was ordained a priest. At the college he managed the financial affairs of the school. In 1838, needing more capital to face the college's outstanding debts, he and other Jesuit leaders were involved in "a tragic and disgraceful affair," i.e., the sale to southern slaveholders of

272 slaves who had been toiling in several Jesuits' Maryland plantations. (See chapter 5 of Robert Emmett Curran's seminal work, *The Bicentennial History of Georgetown University*; and Curran, "Splendid Poverty.") After serving for a time as chaplain in the Mexican war in 1847, he moved to Boston, where he was instrumental in the founding of Boston College.

18. Father Luigi Pellico's (1800–1870) brother Silvio Pellico had been imprisoned by the Austrians in the Spielberg fortress for ten years, from 1820 to 1830, for having participated in a patriotic rebellion organized by the Carbonari. After being released, in 1832, he published *Le mie prigioni* (My Prisons, or My Imprisonment), a moving account of his years spent in confinement. Pellegrino Rossi (1787–1848), who had stayed in Rome during the French upheavals because the pope had appointed him minister of justice of the Papal States met with a tragic end at the hand of an assassin incited by the Roman populace.

19. *Woodstock Letters*, 27, 1; see also Pizzorusso, "Giovanni Antonio Grassi."

20. Garraghan, "John Anthony Grassi"; cited by Daley, Georgetown University, 202.

21. Father Benedict J. Fenwick, SJ, 1817; Father Anthony Kohlmann, SJ, 1817–20; Father Enoch Fenwick, SJ, 1820–25; Father Benedict J. Fenwick, SJ, 1825; Father Stephen Dubuisson, SJ, 1825–26; Father William Feiner, SJ, 1826–29; Father John W. Beschter, SJ, 1829.

22. Dickens, *American Notes*, 1:297–98.

ACKNOWLEDGMENTS

I N THE MANY years this small book was in the making, I have accumulated many debts. First of all, I would like to thank Robert Emmett
Curran for graciously agreeing to write an enlightening foreword and
John C. Hirsh for his encouragement to complete the work and for his liberal constructive criticism. My best thanks go as well to Adam Rothman for
his valuable and insightful comments, to Al Bertrand, Elizabeth Crowley
Webber, and Glenn Saltzman at Georgetown University Press for their
generous and considerate expert advice, and to Alfred Imhoff for his excellent work as the book's copyeditor. My gratitude goes also to the personnel
of the Special Collections Division of the Georgetown University Library
and to the library's staff who helped me with their knowledge and with
locating and putting at my disposal the primary sources I needed. I must
offer many thanks as well to Brian Pals, the present managing editor of
the *North American Review* at the University of Northern Iowa, for helping me identify the author of Father Grassi's unsigned 1823 book review.
I also want to thank the press's two anonymous reviewers, Stephen A.
La Rocca for his key role in the translation of the text, Moyra Byrne for
editing most of the manuscript, and Josiah Osgood, Amy Phillips, and Sally
Vanderhoof, who helped me render in English a few but important Latin
expressions interspersed in Father Grassi's text. Finally, I thank Jacklyn Pi
of the Georgetown University Library's Gelardin New Media Center for
her technical assistance as well as Romeo Sabatini and Maurizio Fontana
for their support.

Notizie

1

News on the Present Condition of the Republic of the United States of Northern America

⟫⟩◦⟨⟪

ALTHOUGH THE UNITED STATES of America has nowadays become the subject of much interest throughout the world, arousing the attention of politicians, merchants, and craftsmen—as well as, above all, those interested in the spread of religion—not many people have an accurate idea of how powerful and vast that empire rising across the Atlantic actually is. After hearing some stories that I told upon my return to Italy from America, several friends expressed the desire that I, having developed a considerable knowledge of those regions during several years' residence there, might put down in writing experiences that an Italian would find noteworthy. Thus I have convinced myself to write down these observations more to appease the requests of friends than from any confidence in my ability to adequately treat this extensive subject, which would require greater skill, ingenuity, and documentation than I possess.

Whatever the merit of this work, I hope that it will not be unworthy of the attention of the reader who wishes to gain greater knowledge of the current state of the North American republic. First I speak of the country's geographic and social conditions, then of its various religious sects, and finally of the current status of the Catholic religion in these territories. I sincerely hope that the courteous reader will give more attention to the information contained herein than to the style and order in which the account is written. It is not my intention to give a complete description of the United States; I simply want to provide a clear picture of that country as it is at the present time. To gain a general idea of its size and situation, the reader may refer to any treatise on modem geography, or even to the appended table (see below). In this work I have sought to describe what most attracted my attention there and what, I hope, most deserves the attention of others.

It is important to note at the outset that the inhabitants of these territories call themselves Americans and their country America, as if Canada and South America were not also really part of America, or their inhabitants not also really Americans. I also continue to use these terms, as to do so is now customary, even in Europe. The Americans also call their country Columbia, and in some literary works they call themselves sons and daughters of Columbia. This they do in honor of Christopher Columbus, and in a certain way to do so makes up for the injustice of naming the land he discovered after Amerigo Vespucci. New England comprises the states of Vermont, Connecticut, Massachusetts, New Hampshire, and Rhode Island, and it is the most highly cultivated and populated region of the United States. When generalizing about the United States, therefore, one needs to make many exceptions with regard to the New England states. I mention this at the beginning to avoid redundancy later on.

CLIMATE

Lying between northern latitudes 26° 50' and 45° 50', the United States do clearly manifest a great variety of climate. Those who base their ideas of a country's climate on its latitude, however, would be deceived in the case of the United States, which exhibits an incredible difference in climate from those areas of Europe that lie in the same latitudes. Washington, the capital of the United States, is at about the same latitude as Lisbon, but it is so cold in the winter that one must wait six months before heat arrives. Sleighs are used, and for weeks the Potomac, the large river on whose banks the city was founded, is covered by ice thick enough to withstand the weight of people and sometimes even of horses and carts. These conditions are unheard of in the capital of Portugal, where the winter resembles a pleasant spring. Toward the north of the United States the cold is more intense, and less intense toward the south; but generally both these areas endure extremes of temperature. The most surprising and uncomfortable aspect of the North American climate are the sudden changes from cold to hot and vice versa, depending on whether the predominating winds are from the south or the northwest. I have experienced the end of a day when the air was pleasant and temperate, and the Potomac was flowing majestically, without a hint of ice; but lo and behold, the following morning the same river was covered with solid ice and the temperature was several degrees below freezing. This phenomenon is commonly attributed to the vastness of the uncultivated land, forests, and great lakes that are found in the northwest. No matter, the older inhabitants claim that the climate is becoming more temperate, and that the winters are not as severe as in the past. Everyone will agree, however, that these rapid climatic changes cannot possibly be good for one's health. In the southern states, during the summer months, fevers are a frequent occurrence; consumption is no less rare in America than in England; and everyone is aware of the distress that yellow fever frequently causes in the southern cities.

Soil

The soil in the United States varies greatly. Toward the Atlantic coast, it is ordinarily alluvial; in the mountains, it is usually meager and light, though rich and fertile in the valleys. The lands of Tennessee, Ohio, and Kentucky attract a large number of settlers each year because they correspond well to their greedy homesteading needs. But since the best land in those states has by now been taken up, a large number of families continue moving onward, beyond the Mississippi, to settle in the state of Missouri.

The price of land varies according to its quality, the number of inhabitants, the proximity of navigable rivers, and other circumstances. A few years ago an acre (which is an area of 43,560 square feet) in Tennessee sold for $4, but with the rush of new settlers the price has risen to $20, $30, and even more. A good map will show the direction of the various mountain chains as well as the great number of large rivers that traverse those immense territories. It was with good reason that European voyagers described the natural phenomena of the New World as having the most gigantic proportions; indeed, one sees there the highest mountains, the largest rivers, and the most extensive bodies of freshwater. It appears to me, however, that this observation does not apply to the fauna of the United States.

Products

Omnis fert omnia tellus (All lands shall bear all fruits) may well be said of the country of which we speak.[1] The primary product of America is grain, and the flour ground from it represents the chief commercial item. Corn is very widely cultivated, and it is used as feed for beasts of burden because the cultivation of hay is largely neglected in various areas. Besides the excellent tobacco, which is well known in every part of Europe, one can find there every type of vegetable, legume, and fruit. Apples and peaches are so abundant that cider is made from the former, and from the latter together with rye, a widely used liquor is distilled. Some Swiss, Italians, and French have made various attempts at cultivating grapes, but so far they have met with little success. Nevertheless, the vine dressers have not become discouraged, and it appears that the wild grapes that grow freely in the woods have provided some hope for future successes in this field. Catholic missionaries, having had difficulty in finding pure wine for use in saying the Holy Mass, have sometimes been able to make a tolerable (yet for them precious) wine from these wild grapes.[2] The wine transported there from Europe is always mixed with too much *aquavitae*, added to help sustain it during its long sea voyage. Moreover, in America, as in England, the arts of adulterating and counterfeiting wine are so refined that even the most intelligent people are sometimes fooled. Olive trees are not yet cultivated in America, but it is believed that they will be successfully grown in the states furthest south, where even mulberries grow without cultivation. I must not forget to mention that from the maple tree, common in the north, a considerable quantity of sugar is harvested. But I should not dwell any longer on this subject, because it is dealt with in the appended table.

The study of agriculture is regarded highly everywhere in the United States. Regarding this point, the northern states, which were first to be settled and are not cultivated by slaves, have a decided superiority over the southern states. In various areas agricultural societies have been formed to encourage this study as well as to sponsor the printing of journals and the publishing of dissertations. Periodically, fairs are held where prizes are given for the best ox, the best wool, or the best agricultural invention. Unenlightened prejudices favoring the retention of antiquated agricultural practices are rarer in that new country than anywhere else. The Americans have not failed to take advantage from the new discoveries of chemistry for improving the land and have judiciously employed lime and clover to enrich the soils when they are turned under. It is true that those soils could be yet more productive; but even with the present scarcity of manual labor, the Americans know how to extract the greatest profit from them.

With regard to food, I can state after having been in almost all the countries of Europe that, in my judgment, no other people in the world are better off than in America, where both meat and fish are found in great abundance. The French who have settled in the United States have rightly observed that there one can see fulfilled the realization of the project hoped for by their own Henry the Fourth: that he should not think himself happy until each of his subjects would have a chicken in his pot every Sunday.³ I cannot say that the United States has been equally provided with a good supply of beverages, which consist merely of whiskey (a sort of *aquavitae*), rum, and other distilled spirits, which are mixed with water for common use. Wine is very expensive, and even beer is still relatively uncommon.

COMMERCE

Commerce and manufacturing are additional sources of civil prosperity for the United States. Everyone knows how extensive the former is: American ships call at ports in the four corners of the globe, in China and India, and around the Baltic and Mediterranean seas, selling their own or others' goods and taking in exchange that which they need or that which they can sell to their advantage elsewhere. The United States' acquisition of Louisiana has opened a new and vast field that is extremely advantageous for its commerce.⁴ It seems that the western states of the Union have received a new life now that they can freely ship their products down the Ohio and Mississippi rivers to New Orleans and, from there, to whatever part of the world they desire. Steamboat traffic has developed to such an extent on the Ohio, the Mississippi, and the other large rivers of the western states that transporting goods from New Orleans to Saint Louis, Louisville, or other cities costs much less than it would from Baltimore, from whence, via Pittsburgh, the merchandise for those states used to be shipped. Thus the invention of these steamships, which has proven to be such a boon to the western part of the United States, has spelled disaster for those ports on the Atlantic that formerly dispatched a great quantity of merchandise.

America's export commerce in flour, tobacco, cotton, lumber, turpentine, and salted fish amounted in 1812 to a value of $45,294,043, which was similar to that of goods imported (namely, clothing, textiles, ironware, coffee, sugar, wine, and liquor), while in 1817 it amounted to $64,728,000.[5] Business endeavors there have been developed to a degree of refinement almost unknown in Europe. Some examples of this are the great number of banks that lend money at interest, insurance offices, and the very tolerant laws regarding business failures, which, although they are very frequent, are not considered dishonorable. The large number of people who have become rich through commerce (not to mention the number who have been ruined by it) inspires and excites in everyone a great ambition and diligence to make money without regard to hardship of labor. Thus, if Americans hear of a place where profits are to be made, they quickly go there, whether it be one extremity or another of the United States, in one hemisphere or the other of the globe. They seemingly have no attachment to where they were born, nor to where they were brought up, but only to where they hope to enrich themselves and make a fortune.

To furnish additional information on the extent of US commerce, one need only mention that, in 1816, 1,191 merchant ships landed at the port of New York alone, and the customs duties paid at the various ports from March 1815 to July 1816 were as follows:

New York	$9,926,188.30
Philadelphia	$5,085,206.65
Boston	$3,579,130.77
Charleston	$1,041,546.73
New Orleans	$732,083.13
Savannah	$521,287.58
Norfolk	$491,150.36

If one glances at the coast of the United States, one notices a great number of ports not mentioned in the foregoing list, each of whose maritime customs offices also provide the government with substantial public revenue. In his address the current president stated that in 1817, the revenue of the United States amounted to $24,500,000, while expenditures were $11,800,000.[6] Additionally, $10 million was used to pay down the public deficit, which has been estimated by some to be $99 million.

The Americans rival the English in the field of manufacturing, whose value in the United States in 1810 was estimated at $120 million. Since then, manufacturing has grown significantly, so in 1816 it was valued at $200 million. Products consist of cotton textiles, rope, clothing, paper, hides and leather, weapons, glass, majolica, potash, tar, and many other things. Factories of every type multiply every day, and Americans hope that soon they will not need to resort to importing foreign products but instead will be in a position to export their own. Machines are commonly used, as in England, but Americans do not suffer the ill effects that are the plight of the English—namely, unemployment, a lack of bread, and poverty resulting from a high population density. Such was the state of the American economy until 1817, when a period of unexpected misfortune befell the nation. I chronicle this occurrence by referring to the account given in the *Historical Review* for 1819, which, I hope, serves as a useful warning to the speculators and planners of our day.

During the last wars between the major powers of Europe, Americans made considerable profits through foreign trade. Nevertheless, many Americans suffered great losses, because no fewer than 917 American ships richly loaded with goods were captured by the British, and more than 1,000 were captured or confiscated by the French. In all, losses amounted to more than $20 million. Facing such losses, American businessmen turned to fictitious capital by means of creating new banks, which began to proliferate at an extraordinary pace all over the United States.

Having begun in commercial US cities, this system soon spread to towns, and from towns it extended even to smaller villages and hamlets. Seeing how easy it was to circulate paper bank coupons secured by undetermined, vague assets, many individuals given to speculation—and even small states—began to take advantage of this opportunity as if it were a gold mine, and thus these coupons multiplied beyond belief. With the value of these holdings apparently appreciating, many believed that they were becoming richer and richer, unaware that their coupons were actually decreasing in value because they were merely paper. Under these conditions, at the beginning, hard work and industriousness were replaced by a strange sort of speculation. Everyone wanted to become wealthy quickly; the prosperous life earned by more modest gains and hard work was looked upon with disdain. Then one witnessed the proliferation of coupon forgers, with the resultant decline in value of the paper and the impoverishment of many. By this point, a sort of unrestrained greed prevailed in all those cities where this dreadful system of paper money predominated. Finally, however, a healthy reaction took place: men recognized that hard work and frugality were indispensable moral virtues in the divine plan, even though, meanwhile, the public had to suffer in proportion to its past madness.

One hears of various proposals to alleviate such disastrous situations, but who will believe that a law passed by his legislative body can have the magical effect of changing the prodigal to frugal, the luxurious to the temperate, and the glorification of pompous ostentation to an honest and just economy?

POPULATION

The first colony in the vast territories that were later to make up the United States was settled in 1610. The first settlers depended on the mother country for all needed manufactured goods and staples. They established their colonies mainly on the Atlantic coast, and the colonies did not extend west of the mountains. Through continuous immigration, the population grew to such an extent that in 1776 it already counted no less than 3 million inhabitants. Until this time the settlements remained merely colonies of England, but, in that same year, under the pretense of demanding certain rights, they rebelled and declared their independence. From then on, there were many changes, the settlements extended beyond the Mississippi and Missouri rivers, and the population grew at a rate unmatched in the history of nations. From the appended table, it is evident that in a brief span of twenty years, the number of inhabitants almost doubled; in 1790 it was 3,884,605, and in 1810 it was 7,239,903.

At this point, allow me to offer a prospective picture of the future greatness of this emerging empire. The area of the United States is estimated at no less than 2,379,350 square miles, and one may figure that every square mile can support about three hundred people. In our projection, we use a figure not higher than a hundred people per square mile; yet with this supposition, the territories of the United States could sustain 240 million inhabitants with a density no higher than that currently found along the Atlantic coast. To give the reader a better understanding of this point, I have added the following table, with which one may compare the actual and possible future population densities of America with those of several European countries.

Number of inhabitants per square mile in Europe

England   118
France   174
Ireland   156
Spain   72
Scotland   63

Number of inhabitants per square mile in America in 1816

Connecticut   60
Massachusetts 54
New York   18
Pennsylvania   16
Virginia   14
Louisiana   2

If the United States were populated like Pennsylvania, they would have 32 million inhabitants; if they had the same density as England, their population would be 236 million; if they had Italy's, they would have 528 million! Having better information upon which to base reasonable conjecture on the future size of the United States, we can move beyond a discussion of mere possibilities. Past facts give us reason to believe that the current population will increase at the same rate as it has in recent years; that is, doubling every twenty years. Therefore, if in 1810 there were 7 million inhabitants, in 1830 there will be 14 million; in 1850, 28 million; in 1870, 56 million; in 1890, 102 million [*sic*]; and at the end of this century, there will be 154 million [*sic*].[7] To show that this is not an unreasonable expectation, I submit this further evidence of the very rapid increase in population and progress of commerce in the United States: in 1790 there were barely 75 post offices, but in 1800 they already numbered 903, growing to 1,230 in 1810 and to 2,977 in 1813.

I could submit many examples of the rapid proliferation of private families, but for the sake of brevity I offer only the following representative case. In the first years after the Revolution, the two brothers Noel, both colonists in Pennsylvania, took wives. One had sixteen children, the other had fifteen. The families grew in such a way that in time they numbered two hundred members, founding a beautiful settlement in the mountains of southern Pennsylvania not far from the mission of Conewago.[8]

About one-seventh of the present population consists of Negroes, who are held as slaves in open contradiction of one of the first articles of the general Constitution of that republic, which declares that liberty is an inherent and inalienable right of man. I cannot deny, however, that there are some good reasons for not granting freedom all at once to Negroes. One should not get the idea, however, that the American shores continue to be afflicted by the sight of ships landing unhappy victims of human greed. The Negroes found in the United States are the descendants of those Africans who in the past were transported to the New World colonies from their native countries. The importation of foreign slaves is strictly prohibited today, but, in spite of these measures, the greedy still often succeed in continuing to trade in slaves. In fact, the traffic in those poor people within the country is still permitted by civil law. Men are sold to men, and in the land of liberty one often hears the mournful sound of the rattling of slave chains. In many states of the Union, Negroes are treated well and are better nourished than European peasants, but in many others they are left in total ignorance of religion, no attention is paid to their morals, and they are neither baptized nor encouraged to unite in the sacred bonds of matrimony. The greedy master cares only that they work hard. As far as the rest, he allows them to follow the blind, brutish impulses of their passions and to also practice their magic and superstitions, which are beyond belief. This occurs mainly in the South; in the northern states slavery has been abolished, and this example is, little by little, being imitated in the other states as well.

Many Europeans imagine that a large proportion of Americans are civilized native Indians. This is a mistaken notion, for the population is almost totally made up of European families—English, Irish, Germans, French, and others. It is worthwhile to note how these people generally came into possession of the land. It is very different from the way in which the Spanish took over South America, or the way in which the English came into possession of a good portion of the East Indies. The settlers gained possession not by a violent invasion with swords drawn but through the means of amicable treaties with the Indians, who ceded or sold hundreds of square miles of their land and withdrew further inland, beyond several rivers. This was how Lord Baltimore established the colony of Catholics in Maryland and, likewise, how William Penn founded Pennsylvania for the Quakers. Through these treaties, the United States possesses 150 million acres of uncultivated land situated east of the

Mississippi River that may be sold to individuals, and perhaps as many additional acres west of that river.

It is useful to describe how land is sold and how the government plans parcel out this land to industrious settlers who desire clear title, providing public revenue for the Republic and preventing monopolies at the same time. The plan is as follows. Before the land ceded by the Indians to the government is put up for sale, it is measured by order of the public authority and divided into townships, which are further subdivided into sections. Each township measures 6 square miles and is divided into 36 sections, each 1 square mile in area. Each section contains 640 acres and is distinguished by a number, from 1 to 36. Because section number 16 is situated near the center, it is designated for the building of a school. The three adjacent sections are reserved for government, although they may be sold in the future, pending approval by Congress. In Washington, the headquarters of the federal government of the United States, there is a general bureau for land sales; and in each district in which these lands are located, there are subordinate bureaus that deal with the sale of land. The minimum quantity that the government sells is 160 acres, costing $2 per acre, half to be paid in cash, the other half to be paid in four years. If one pays the whole amount in cash, the price of an acre is only $1.64.

This is the plan. But let us turn our attention to its effects. Every industrious person able to pay the reasonable sum of $80 can freely own the land, and, although he may be otherwise without money, he can succeed in paying the balance due within four years by selling the lumber from the trees cut to clear the land for cultivation. First, he must take into consideration the long trek to the land and procure some livestock, simple tools, and all else that will be necessary to sustain his homestead until the first harvest from his land. In such a way he becomes a peaceful landowner, having but a trifling sum to pay (which is proportionate to what he owns), and thus he can lead a happy life. This is one of the principal reasons why the US population grows at such an excessive rate. A father of a large family gives a small amount of money to his adult sons, who move further inland and buy and work the land there, becoming able to support themselves, their wives, and their children. Those on the coast who can barely make a living, by selling their small farms are enabled to buy farms ten times larger with the money they receive, and these larger parcels are more suited to the needs of their families.

Some people have spread various rumors of the good fortune of those who have immigrated to America; some say that the government gave free land, tools, houses, and so on to newly arrived colonists. With these expectations, many went to the New World and paid the price for their greedy ingenuousness. They found themselves thoroughly discouraged and in great despair, but this did not always last long, because every industrious man can easily provide for himself there. Those who would ever consider such a venture, however, should well appraise their own situation, and the Italians, especially, should bear in mind the proverb *Chi sta bene non si muova* (Those who are doing well should remain where they are). Even if the wave of European emigration were to turn to the best climate and most fertile shores of South America, the population of the northern United States would still keep increasing due to the system in effect and the spirit driving its inhabitants.

The reader will readily perceive the difference between the life of colonists who settle in the wilderness and of those living in cities, or in territories that have already been settled. The new settlers start out by living in log cabins, which are houses of beam and rafter construction. Their fissures are plugged with stones and mud, making these cabins barely sufficient to protect against inclement weather. But as the settlers prosper, they build frame houses made with joists and small beams, and with in-between sections made of bricks set in mortar and whitewashed. These homes are kept very neat and clean. One must note that even in the city, the servants' quarters, the kitchen, the storeroom, the stable, *le lieu d'aisance* (the toilet), the granary, and the meat pantry are usually separate or detached from the house where the masters reside. When the settlers become well off, they construct houses made entirely of brick, and these are what one usually sees in cities great and small. American cities have the rare advantage of being built from well-conceived and uniform plans. The streets are very wide and straight, and occasionally the main roads are lined by poplar trees. Unlike those in most European cities, both sides of the streets have convenient sidewalks that spare the pedestrian the aggravation of dodging horses, carriages, and carts.

To give a better idea of an American city, I now make some observations about the new city of Washington, the seat of the federal government of the United States. Washington's foundation was decreed in 1791, after serious disturbances in Philadelphia by the Pennsylvania militia, which had been gathered there at the time that Congress was convening in that city. These armed soldiers dared to surround the assembly room and demanded with threats that funds be allocated at once to cover the back pay that was due them. Congress immediately moved to New York, and there, after reflecting on the danger of similar menaces and the need for freedom and order to deliberate the common interests of the republic, it resolved to build a new city that would be exempt from such interferences. General George Washington, then president of the United States, was charged with the task of selecting a tract of land that he thought would be most opportune for this purpose. He chose an area of 10 miles square on the borders of Maryland and Virginia, which was then named Columbia. This territory was declared independent from any other state and subject only to Congress. Under General Washington's supervision, the plan of the city that was to bear his name was laid out.

The main streets are 140 to 160 feet wide and, in the manner of avenues, divided into three parts: the middle lane is used for carts and animals of every sort, and the two lateral parts are used by pedestrians. One finds the most significant public buildings along these avenues, the principal one being the Capitol. This is situated on a most pleasant hill and is composed of a large central body flanked by two large wings, all in the Corinthian style. Its construction was begun in 1793, and General Washington had the pleasure of laying the first stone. About a mile west of the Capitol, one finds the house of the president, built in the Ionic style. On its four sides are located the buildings housing the Department of the Navy, the War Department, the Department of State, and the Department of the Treasury. Other important buildings are the shipyard, where warships are constructed and repaired; the post office; the patent office, for new inventions; and a small fort on the Potomac.[9]

From place to place, there are public squares or piazzas to improve the circulation of the air. In the surrounding area there is a variety of pleasant hills that are very suitable for country homes. Tiber Creek empties into a canal that was dug across the city in 1811 connecting with the Potomac.[10]

Whatever some people may say, it seems that Washington will never become a large metropolis, although it is the capital of a vast empire. Commerce in the city is minimal because Baltimore on one side and Alexandria and Georgetown on the other offer more convenient port services for the distribution of goods. Since the government is republican, it does not attract those gentlemen who elsewhere enjoy staying in the area of the residence of a court. The city already has a supply of housing sufficient for the lodgings of government workers, foreign ministers, congressional representatives, and those who come from other places for business. Thus it certainly will not continue to grow at the pace that it has in recent years. Except for several government buildings and banks, the architecture in the other cities is simple and monotonous. The facades of the houses are of red-painted brick intercalated with small layers of white mortar. In the rooms one does not see paintings, statues, or gilt furniture; but one may see mahogany furniture, a few pretty copperware pieces, or beautiful rugs on the floor. If the Italian magnificence is lacking, there is an atmosphere of comfort, simplicity, and cleanliness that is not easy to describe. In city houses, window panes, floors, and even thresholds are washed at least once a week. Building construction is usually very weak because of the great quantity of lumber that is used. This is one of the causes of the frequent fires there—but firefighting efforts are quick and efficacious. Every neighborhood has night watchmen, and they have established a system whereby designated men equipped with pumps, ladders, buckets, and other useful tools quickly respond to the first fire alarm. In New York, which is along a river, in order to quickly provide water for the machines, a series of these pumps are set up in an instant, drawing water from the river and transmitting it from one pump to the next through leather tubes until it reaches the burning house.

Large multifamily dwellings like those found in Italy are unknown. Houses in the United States are constructed in such a way that they are used exclusively by only one family, with rooms on top of other rooms instead of being arranged on the same floor. If one wishes to have a large house, then two are put together to form one, as there are always internal communicating doorways made for this purpose. Americans find it strange that in Europe one family will live on the first floor, another family will live on the second, and another on the third floor of the same house. And they find it even stranger that horses and carriages exit from the same building. In American cities there are not the squares, arcades, fountains, or other ornaments that are commonly seen in Italy. But water is very abundant there, and many public drinking fountains and underground canals supply houses. To maintain public quietness and cleanliness, slaughterhouses are located outside the city, and meat to be sold is brought in to shops or to the market, which is held in a sort of arcade built for that use. Public order and quietness are generally well maintained. Bread is so abundant that there are few thieves, and one does not see poor people or beggars in public. I say "in public" because many tradesmen usually spend all the money they make, and if they become invalid they are reduced to the most deplorable misery.

The language that is universally spoken is English, which has not yet been corrupted into a variety of dialects as it has in England. Weights and measures are according to the English system. The monetary system is decimal, the dollar being equivalent to the Spanish piece.[11] People often make use of bank coupons to avoid the inconvenience of carrying cash. Since trade has stagnated and various banks have failed, however, these coupons no longer enjoy the trust they once had.

Character

It is difficult to portray the character of the United States, because the nation has not yet exhibited a specific one, and every part of the United States shows European traces, which is only natural because the first and the most numerous settlements were derived from Europe. Thus one encounters French vivacity, British seriousness, Irish hospitality, and German industriousness. But, generally speaking, as a result of the language and customs, English character still predominates. Because various nations have established settlements there, it is not surprising that towns and cities in the New World have been given names like London, Oxford, Dublin, Paris, and Amsterdam. The nature of the republican government is such that some places are given names like Sparta, Athens, Utica, Rome, and even Tiber and Capitol. In general, one notices a republican deportment in the people, who are proud of their freedom and oppose any subjugation external to their own laws. This pride is seen in even the poorest people, who respond in a stand-offish manner when questioned. A barefoot, impudent wretch spoke in the following unrestrained manner: "Do you want to give me a pair of shoes?" A wage earner would be offended if someone mentioned that he works for a master instead of saying that he helps said master. If one would ask him, "Where is your master?" he would immediately respond, "I don't have a master," meaning that he is not a slave. Nevertheless, perhaps the most distinctive American character is being *indocilis pauperiem pati* (untaught to endure poverty), placing avidity for profit on a par with industry.

There are numerous associations for building roads, canals, and bridges, and for promoting commerce and manufacturing. Letters are diligently delivered from one end of the United States to the other. A series of couriers has been established from Anson, Maine, to Nashville, a distance of 1,448 miles from northeast to southwest. There is another series from Saint Mary's, Georgia, to Highgate, Vermont, a distance of 1,369 miles in a south–north direction. At least this was the situation by 1818. These couriers pass through the city of Washington. There is always a large number of wayfarers, and all means are used to make traveling more comfortable and facilitate the expeditious transporting of merchandise. There are many stagecoaches, and their departures and arrivals are well regulated. Hotels are usually clean and comfortable. What can I say then of the "steam boats"—that is, boats powered by steam—the "team boats"—that is, boats powered by horses that ride on same—and the "mail boats" that run from city to city in such great number? I must not forget to mention that the great canal decreed by the New York legislature will soon be completed; it will connect the Hudson River, which flows into the ocean at New York City, with the Great Lakes—Superior, Michigan, Huron, Erie, and Ontario. A quick glance at a good map will instantly show the immense advantages to be derived from the completion of such a work.

Among the inhabitants of the United States, those of New England are regarded as the most cunning and clever, capable of ingenious deceptions; they are called Yankees. The number of small entrepreneurs who originate in New England and spread to all the other states and make profits by any possible means has given rise to this concept of Yankees. The English have extended this name indiscriminately to all Americans. One obviously must use extreme care and farsightedness and be familiar with their commercial laws to deal with such people. But in my opinion, it is unjust to give all Americans a label that should only be attributed to individuals or at the most to a single class of people.

Customs

The prevalence of unrestrained liberty, the frequent drunkenness, the rabble of so many adventurers, the numerous Negroes who are kept in slavery, the large number of sects that prevail and the little that is known of the true religion there, the large number of sensationalistic novels that are read, and the insatiable greed for wealth—all these circumstances adversely affect one's idea of American customs. At first sight, one does not see the bad things found in the country, for they are often hidden beneath a well-composed exterior. But they are not hard to see through once one becomes familiar with the people, especially in the cities. The vices of gambling and drinking are more prevalent there than anyone in Italy could imagine, and the consequences are fatal for individuals and entire families. The people are generally civil; but through this civility, one can notice in many a lack of good manners—for example, cutting one's nails or combing one's hair in the presence of others, putting one's feet upon another chair while sitting, or bracing them up against a wall are not considered indecorous. When an American introduces a stranger to acquaintances, he points to each acquaintance while naming him. Friends seeing each other, even after many years, do not usually embrace but shake hands. Mothers have the admirable habit of nursing their own babies, but many would be even more worthy of praise if they did it with greater modesty. The custom of swaddling babies has entirely ceased in the United States. Those born there have a rather weak constitution, and yet one rarely sees crippled or deformed people. Even well-to-do people do not disdain using the ploughshare or the spade in the fields, and they even eat there with the laborers. Luxury in dressing has reached a level that is perhaps hardly known in Europe. In the country, people dress almost as well as they do in the city, and on holidays it is quite impossible to judge a person's financial status by the clothes he wears. The most usual form of entertainment for Americans is dancing, and it appears that their mania for jumping about is no less than that of the French.

Frequent duels are caused by people's honor being sullied. To avoid the rigor of the law, the duelers usually head to the frontier of a neighboring territory to settle their quarrels. This barbarous, foolish, and superstitious custom usually ends with the transgressor winning, leaving the innocent party furthermore unjustly wounded, crippled, or killed. Until now, the many fatalities from dueling have not influenced the public authority to use greater severity in suppressing this madness. These duels have also been fatal for the republic. Alexander Hamilton, who succeeded the great Washington as commander of the Continental Army, was lost in this way in a duel with Aaron Burr, who was vice president of the United States.[12] A monument was erected at the place where Hamilton fell, and to this day the site is the field of battle for New York duelers. In 1815 two young officers in Virginia lost their lives in a pistol duel, which is the most common type of duel. These are the fine results stemming from so-called affairs of honor. Such a serious disruption seems to have recently caused a reaction in public sentiment. Toward the end of 1821 a member of Congress proposed a law that would effectively prevent the occurrence of duels, but the outcome of such a wise and Christian proposal is not yet known.[13]

Observers of American customs have often deplored the indulgence that the father of a family shows toward his children, knowing neither how to contradict them nor how to constrain their capricious desires. This attribute is most prevalent in the southern states. Nevertheless, education, especially the sort that is practical for making a decent living and to advance, is far from being neglected. Also, to facilitate the education of the poor, relatives and guardians are authorized by law to place youngsters under the supervision of a tradesman, who is obligated to maintain them until the age of twenty-one, teaching them his trade, together with reading, writing, and counting. The laws regarding this important benefit for public welfare are very strict.[14]

To show how highly regarded education is there, one need only say that sometimes a father uses all the money of the portion allotted to a particular son for that son's education. A wealthy farmer will support a son at the university while keeping another at his side with the plough. Some young people of limited means spend the winter attending elementary school in the country until they are able to save enough money to support themselves in the summer studying the sciences at a boarding school. The literary education is of two kinds: classical and simple English. The first includes Greek and Latin literature, rhetoric, mathematics, and various branches of philosophy; this is for those aspiring to the bar or medicine. The latter is for those destined for agriculture or commerce, and consists of the study of correct writing and reading of the language, arithmetic, a little geography, and other cognate subjects. In New England a law requires every town of at least fifty families to maintain a public school.

The Lancaster type of school is very common in America.[15] When these schools were first introduced, even upper-class people sent their children to them, but they had to remove them quickly because of the depraved habits and crude manners that their children were picking up from association with a base and crass group of fellow students. The education of girls rarely consists only of learning sewing, spinning, and working with flax and wool. But after they complete the English school, they never fail to learn to dance, and they sometimes take lessons in music on the harpsichord, drawing, and perhaps even French, thus completing their education. It does not matter that after a few weeks all is forgotten; for their vanity, it is enough just to be able to say that they studied music, drawing, and French. European teachers working in America often admire the docility and modesty of the children studying at boarding schools with regular discipline (assuming the children have not been spoiled before they enter the school). To these attributes one must add a certain frankness, mature behavior, and common sense, qualities that one rarely sees elsewhere. But nobler thoughts and sentiments of unselfishness, generosity, honor, and gratitude are seldom encountered in those born and raised in the country among Negroes. The inconstancy of goodness in the young seems to be a trait more common in America than in other countries, and one often experiences the pain of seeing the most encouraging hopes betrayed by the most dreadful changes. When American children reach a certain age, they grow restless and impatient with being subjugated unless they are disciplined with a strong hand. From the arrogation of liberties they frequently pass on to insubordination, and at times they even rebel violently against their superiors. This is not uncommon in American colleges, occurring in 1816 at Princeton in New Jersey and at William & Mary in Virginia. Revolting students broke windows, desks, furniture, and everything they could get their hands on, and they were about to set fire to the college itself. Unlike most honest Americans, who disapprove excess of licentiousness, many of the authorities that preside over such places are only concerned with imparting some knowledge to their pupils and are not seriously concerned with their misbehaving.

LITERATURE

Romani pueri longis rationibus assem
Discunt in partes centum diducere...
... Haec, animos aerugo, et cura peculi.
Cum semel imbuerit, speramus carmina fingi
Posse linenda cedro, et levi servanda cupresso?

[Our Romans, by many a long sum, learn in childhood how to divide the as into a hundred parts[16]...
... When once this canker, this lust of petty gain has stained the soul, can

we hope for poems to be fashioned, worthy to be smeared with cedar-oil,
and kept in polished cypress?]
—Horace, *Satires, Epistles, and Ars Poetica*, 476–79

This observation by Horace has been confirmed by the evidence in
America, where the commercial spirit and the seeking of wealth charac-
terize every class of people. It should not be surprising, however, to see
rare flowers of poetic genius bloom on the American Parnassus. Learned
men are not lacking there, but perhaps more regard is given to the mere
multiplicity of knowledge than to profound specialization in a single discipline. A certain superficial, scientific affectation is perhaps more widespread and common in America than elsewhere. A truly learned person
would be surprised to hear the confident and decisive tones in which one
there speaks about whatever subject. There is not a house that lacks books
of instruction, literary narratives, and novels; and even if one misses there
the Bible or a catechism, one always finds gazettes. These gazettes are the
most ordinary sources of education in America. They are universal ency-
clopedias that deal with every subject; they are tribunals of the literary
controversies brought before public judgment, heralds that announce all
that occurs in the four corners of the globe, that inform about war and
treaties of peace, commerce, government spending, court sentences, the
prices of every kind of merchandise, all the misfortunes that occur in the
country, deaths, marriages, inventions, and so on.

Sometimes a European can barely contain his indignation or laughter
upon reading on the same page an enthusiastic praise of liberty together
with an announcement of a man's intention to buy or sell so many slaves;
or that such and such a Negro is in prison because of an attempted escape
from a "hero of freedom." The number of gazettes that are printed is incredible; and to encourage their circulation, the government charges only
1 cent to deliver one large paper up to a distance of 100 miles. The conser-
vation of a rather pure form of English, even among the common people,
has been attributed to this continuous, widespread reading of gazettes.
Because of this reading, one of the most frequent topics of conversation
is politics, and each person thinks and speaks according to the gazette he
reads. Scientific and other miscellaneous journals are printed, but rarely
does the same journal continue for many years. One of the better journals
in this respect is the *Edinburgh Review*, from England, which is reprinted
in New York.

Greek literature and Latin literature are commonly studied, but with few exceptions not to such an extent as to permit an understanding and appreciation of the original masterpieces of the great Greek and Italian masters. How else would it be possible that in their publications they place the *Columbiad* by Joel Barlow on the same level or higher than Homer or Virgil, or the speeches of their public representatives on a higher level than the eloquence of Demosthenes or Cicero. One would not deny that Americans express themselves with much facility and refinement, and that occasionally one encounters beautiful and eloquent passages. Only gold is idolized more than an eloquent speech. But of all the aspects that the great masters agree make up the art of speaking well, it is elocution that Americans study most assiduously. As long as one speaks and writes choice expressions and harmonious and elegant phrases, he is considered a great orator, however deficient he may be in new ideas, noble thoughts, seriousness and force of argument, consistency of comportment, or ability to master passions, which would be required elsewhere. I have on several occasions challenged those who praise American eloquence to provide me with a single complete discourse that might be presented credibly to a cultured Europe or left to posterity, an example demonstrating the advanced extent to which the art of speaking has reached across the Atlantic in our day. But not one such discourse has been presented to me, and often, when a work was suggested by some to be a masterpiece, it was rejected by others as being of little importance.

There is a large number of medical students in all parts of the United States, but it should be pointed out that the usual distinction between the northern and southern states also exists here regarding excellence in this field. In the northern states there are sensible regulations governing the study and practice of medicine. In the southern states a young person can become a doctor simply by studying for a period of time with a certified doctor. What would seem strangest to Italians is that medical doctors also act as druggists, and one can well imagine how much they charge for their medicines. The United States prides itself on having produced a Dr. Rush, whose works are highly esteemed in all of Europe.[17]

The material side of literature is far more advanced than one in Italy would think. Printing shops are numerous there, and their presses issue books of admirable elegance and ornamentation. The edition of the Latin authors being printed in Boston, Alexander Wilson's Philadelphia publication *American Ornithology* with its beautiful color plates, and Barlow's

Columbiad are good examples, and these will remain monuments to the excellence of American typography.[18] The traffic in books is very brisk. Circulating libraries are quite common; these lend books in their collections for a given period of time for a set fee. But the books that circulate most, unfortunately, are those novels that deprave the mind and the heart. Several public libraries have been started. To this day, the one in Philadelphia is the largest, and that of the college of Cambridge is said to be well furnished with books. When an Italian hears that the library of the federal government in Washington cost $24,000, he has high expectations; but were he to see and examine it, he would be disillusioned!

Italian literature, which is widely appreciated in England, is almost unknown in America. I believe that this is a result of the lack of communication between that country and Italy, but perhaps it is due more to the prejudice of the sectarians against the Catholic Church. In fact, Protestant ministers continue to represent Italy as a country that groans in the throes of slavery and is kept in blind ignorance by popish superstition. The captains of the ships that call at Italian ports do not see the covered piers common in their own country, they do not commonly find the superficial scientific knowledge that they are used to, and, what is more, they find truly scandalous the nudity to be seen in paintings, engravings, and statues. (This nudity is also condemned by Italian Catholics, but effective measures for eliminating it have not been adopted.) The captains soon conclude, and report to others, that misery, ignorance, and licentiousness are widespread in Italy. *The Classical Tour in Italy*, by the Reverend Abbot Eustace, an impartial British writer, ought to do much to correct these false notions.[19] This book was reprinted in Philadelphia and has been widely applauded by the American public. I hope that the reports of unbiased travelers will also contribute to setting the record straight. Italy has already had the pleasure of having its libraries, cities, and museums visited by cultured young Americans who, while traveling, have no other aim than to broaden their ideas, refine their taste, and acquire knowledge.

Painting, sculpture, and the other purely ornamental arts, however, are in their infancy in the United States, though they are spoken of with respect and admiration. Thus, when Virginians wished to erect a monument to their fellow citizen, the celebrated General Washington, to embellish the Capitol at Richmond, the capital of the state, they turned to none other than the immortal Canova. He consented to their request, and in Rome he carved a statue in marble worthy of the chisel of Phidias. The American hero is represented in ancient garb, courtly in demeanor, in the act of writing his *Valedictory Address* to the United States as he retires from public life to a life of honorable leisure.[20] One of Canova's students, under his supervision, executed on the four walls of the statue's pedestal four bas-reliefs depicting four of the most memorable undertakings of the great Washington. Perhaps this beautiful work is already being admired in America; it will be useful in spreading good taste and refinement in that vast territory. There are academies of the fine arts in New York and Philadelphia, and the success that two Americans, West and Trumbull, have had in painting is proof enough that the natives of the United States are not lacking in the genius needed to succeed in the liberal arts if they wish to cultivate them. The philosophical society established in Philadelphia in 1769 is already known to the cultured of Europe for its *Transactions*, which have been published for some time.

The sciences that are of immediate usefulness are highly promoted in America. Mathematics—even in its most refined branches, physics, mineralogy, and chemistry—is taught by professors of rare merit. Until now, the study of astronomy has not developed there to the extent that one would expect from a population with so many great navigators, and Americans have contented themselves with reprinting the *Nautical Almanac* for use by their navy. People well versed in the theory and practice of this highly esteemed science are not lacking there, and, if it is encouraged and promoted, it will lend new distinction to their empire. The work of Nathaniel Bowditch on practical navigation and the various pamphlets and journal articles by Adrian and Wallace prove my assertion.[21] It is said that the government has already acquired astronomical instruments of excellent quality. The lack of these has, so far, prevented exact computation of the longitude of the city of Washington. The measurement—which has been deduced from various observations, however, and which appears to be accurate—is said to be 76° 55' 24." west of Greenwich. The research that many are attempting on perpetual motion at least shows the spirit that predominates in the United States, even if it does not yet give glory to their mechanical knowledge. In the surveying of land, Americans make much use of the magnetic needle, but the little attention they give to its variations will become a source of many future quarrels—to which, alas, they are unfortunately too much inclined.

The scarcity of labor impels American ingenuity to invent mechanical devices. To encourage this, a patent office was established in Washington. Inventors are given the exclusive right to the use or sale of their machines, and they are obligated to present models of these, which are subsequently kept in the patent office to satisfy the public's curiosity. Through all of 1819, 101 patents for new inventions were expedited by this office, with the advantage, at least, of receiving a $33 fee for each patent handled. One cannot deny that, among the great number of these models, there are many of considerable ingenuity. One worthy of particular attention is the water saw, which is designed in such a way that one need only secure the log in place and set the saw in motion to have all the boards sawn without the use of one's hands. Another device that elicits much interest is a machine that cuts wire into pieces, bends them, and inserts them in leather, thereby in a short time making identical carding tools. The construction of mills is also very ingenious, resulting in almost all the hard work of milling being done away with.

Before leaving this subject, I must relate what happened to one industrious farmer. When he applied for his patent and presented his model, the model was found to be the well-known screw of Archimedes. Upon hearing that this was not a new invention and seeing an illustration of the same device in an old book, the good man replied ingenuously that he had never known of the screw of Archimedes, that he had invented it, and that no other man in the world had any part in it. The gazettes of 1817 even announced the invention of a machine to teach Latin.

To the honor of the United States, I must mention here that Robert Fulton, an American, was, in 1808, the first to invent the steam engine, a vapor pump used to propel boats. The patent he received for it continues to provide a substantial income to his surviving family. In passing, I must note that the Englishman Ferguson states that one Pancas, an Italian, was the first to observe and make known to others that the expanding vapor produced by heat could be harnessed to produce movement. This inspired the invention of the "pompes a feu," which later became the steam engine.[22]

The art for which the Americans are recognized as masters even by their rivals is that of ship construction, especially of vessels used in transporting merchandise. Americans are able to combine ideally aesthetic qualities and the best advantage of form with those elements making for maneuverability, so their ships perform excellently with a minimum number of sailors. They would take the prize over all others if the woods they used in construction were of greater durability. This defect is said to be due to the lack of certain oleaginous substances in the lumber that they use in their building. To conclude this subject, I relate an interesting article in the Roman gazette *Le notizie del giorno* for November 21, 1816:

> A steam frigate was recently launched at New York of 300 feet in length, with a beam of 200 feet and drawing 13 feet, constructed of oak and cork. It carries 48 guns. In the case of an enemy attempting to board, the frigate can discharge 100 buckets per minute of boiling water from the quarterdeck. With the same mechanism, it can rotate 300 sabers on each side with perfect regularity, and four times a minute it can with an indescribable force hurl halberds which immediately retract to be launched again.

This is the state of the art of mechanics in the United States. The construction of similar frigates was ordered after New York experimental maneuvers satisfied public expectations and confirmed the idea that such vessels would be invincible in defending the ports in which they are stationed. The US Navy in 1820 was composed of four ships of seventy-four guns, nine frigates of thirty-six or more guns, and about forty other vessels of varying strength, which for the most part mount fewer than twenty guns. In the United States there are six shipbuilding yards, found in the following cities: Portsmouth, New Hampshire; Charlestown, Massachusetts; [name not given], Long Island, New York; Philadelphia, on the banks of the Delaware River; Washington, on a branch of the Potomac; and Gosport, on the Elizabeth River in Virginia.[23]

GOVERNMENT

The government of the United States is that of a federal republic. Each state is a small republic with its own constitution, but all the states are bonded together through the federal Constitution to form a large republic, which they call the Union, or the United States. The legislative power rests with Congress, which is made up of the House of Representatives and the Senate. Executive power rests with the president. Every two years the people elect the representatives. Senators are elected every six years, and the president every four years, but by a different method from that used for the House. The Constitution forever guarantees freedom of speech, press, and religion. All people are equal in the eyes of the law, and titles and hereditary distinctions are prohibited. Therefore neither the president, senators, nor justices have distinctive dress or bear emblems of their dignity, and even during public ceremonies they dress as ordinary citizens. When presidents reach the end of the term of office prescribed by the Constitution, they usually retire to leisurely private lives on their estates, in imitation of the immortal Washington, who first gave such a noble example of republican magnanimity. Trial by jury is preserved inviolable. The jury is a court of law composed of twenty-four persons obligated by oath to investigate and judge, basing their decision on evidence given by the testimony of witnesses, who also act under oath. I will not dwell further on the US government, because there are many books that treat this subject in minute detail. In passing, I note that their flag is distinguished by thirteen alternating red and white stripes, and in 1820 there were twenty-two stars in a blue field. It is interesting to note that, when a new state is incorporated into the Union, a new star is added to the flag on the 4th of July following that incorporation.

I must also add that in the abovementioned elections, a candidate seeking votes, both in his speeches and in the press, commonly uses intrigues, deceit, trickery, and pledges, along with gifts of money, whiskey (i.e., *aquavitae*), rum, and other liquors. It is known that the American people are divided into two parties, being called Federalists or Democrats. Both parties support the republican form of government; they dissent only on the way that it is, or should be, administered. On various issues they are united in their opinions, particularly on that of the navy. The illustrious and glorious success that it had in the last war against the English reconciled their disagreements, and they are both eager to maintain it at the highest possible level. Half the public newspapers are Federalist, the other half are Democrat, and neither half spares any punches with regard to the other. The party that prevails never fails to strengthen itself further by distributing public offices to party members, who are often not the most meritorious of men. Conversely, this has led to the practice of using the party for personal speculation.

From this and other circumstances, pessimistic politicians claim that the United States cannot last long under the present system. Certainly toward the end of the last war, one often heard talk of the northern states' inclination to separate from the Union. Others echo the same pessimism, stating that the United States lacks one of the best sources of civil concord:

the bond with religion. They see the fatal seed of future discord in the wide variety of sects, analogous to the jealousy that certain smaller states have toward larger, more powerful ones. Thus, large and wealthy Virginia, which has given the country all its presidents except one, is already looked upon with distrust by many other states.

But others answer that, although there is no universally prescribed religion, one cannot, nevertheless, say that the United States is without religion. In fact, the pseudo philosophism currently so widespread in Europe, which tends to degrade man to the level of a brute, has not made such progress in America, where religion is universally considered not only useful but also necessary for the public good. The belief in the Sacred Scripture and God as rewarder of the good and punisher of the evil in the hereafter is very common. Congress has its own chaplain, changing from one sect to another, and prayers are recited before each congressional session.[24] The president of the Republic and the governors of the states have set aside one day each year to pray and give thanks to the Supreme Provider of every good for the prosperity of those territories. Ultimately, the civil laws in a certain way add much to the maintenance of moral order, public decency, and honesty. Because there are no legal provisions for primogeniture or trusts, and because brothers and sisters equally divide their parental inheritance, it is difficult for one individual to accumulate great wealth. Others share this view, although they are aware that an excessive luxury is becoming evident and is growing. They say that ambition will be contained, and the system will continue to function, as long as the country remains sparsely populated, with its people occupied in clearing land, building houses, and establishing profitable businesses in manufacturing, commerce, and agriculture. These conditions are not conducive to the accumulation of great wealth; but when they end, and rich, ambitious men of great talent and credit emerge, what will become of the Republic across the Atlantic? Different times, personalities, and circumstances call for different forms of government.

With good reason, several wise Americans were amused by violent attempts by French "clubs" in 1788 to establish a republican form of government. What was to be the result of so much bloodshed, suffering, and cruelty? In fact, those same Frenchmen passed from the blindest fanaticism for liberty to the vilest and most abject slavery, thus creating a despicable image in the eyes of true lovers of liberty. But even admitting the correctness of this position, its conclusion belongs to a remote era, and, therefore, it will not be surprising if, as time goes by, the United States suffers the same fate as the world's other republics. I do not present references here to political opinions and their conjectures on the future of America because my intention is to speak only of the current state of that Republic.

In keeping with this aim, I conclude by referring to several particulars of the city of New York, from which the reader may judge in proportion other cities, such as Philadelphia, Boston, and Baltimore. In New York there are nine banks, each with capital of between $200,000 and $2 million, and there are seven insurance companies, each with capital of $500,000.

I add here a list of the establishments of science and of charitable institutions:

1. Association of Doctor and Surgeons
2. Medical-Surgical Society
3. Medical Society
4. American Society of Aesculapius
5. Physio-Medical Society
6. Literary Philosophical Society
7. Historical Society
8. American Society of the Arts
9. Society to Promote the Useful Arts in the State of New York
10. Library Society
11. Emancipation Society
12. Bellevue House for the Poor
13. Philological Society
14. Society to Promote Manufacturing
15. Charity Society
16. Humanity Society
17. Society of Public Schools
18. Washington Society
19. New England Society
20. Society of Mechanics
21. Navy Society
22. Tammany Order (named after the chief and the lineage from which the American Indians originated)
23. French Charity Society
24. Irish Friendly Society

25. German Society
26. New York Hospital
27. Dispensary

Extract from a letter dated January 7, 1812, from Dr. Mitchill to Congressman Thomas Newton, published in *Emporium of Arts and Sciences* by Coxe, Philadelphia, May 1812, no. 1, p. 88. In the state of New York alone, there are these manufacturers:

Tanneries	867
Distilleries	492
Breweries	42
Looms	33,068
Fulling-mills	467
Gunpowder factories	2
Wind furnaces	11
Air furnaces	10
Carding machines	413
Cotton manufacturers	26
Paper factories	28
Hat factories	124
Glass factories	6
Nail factories	44
Forges	48

The letter quoted above also provides the number of sheep in different states: Vermont, 450,000; Massachusetts, 309,182; Connecticut, 400,000; Pennsylvania, 1,466,918. The number of spinning machines operated and owned by private families is incredible. The amount of saltpeter made in the United States is as follows: 59,175 pounds in Virginia, 201,937 in Kentucky, 23,600 in Massachusetts, and 162,425 in Tennessee. I mentioned that sugar is harvested from the maple tree. Here are the quantities: 3,023,806 pounds in Ohio; 2,441,647 pounds in Kentucky; 1,200,000 pounds in Vermont; and 162,340 pounds in eastern Tennessee. Vermont produces 8,000 pounds per year of vitriol, and Tennessee produces 56,000 pounds.

The value of straw hats manufactured every year in Massachusetts amounts to $579,228, and $270,100 worth are made in Connecticut.

The annual value of comb manufacturing is as follows: $30,624 in Massachusetts, $70,000 in Connecticut, and $6,240 in Pennsylvania. Dr. Mitchill has also presented the following figures: cotton spinning wheels, powered by water or horses, number no less than 330, with 100,000 spindles, and are capable of spinning an amount of cotton sufficient to weave 18 million yards on a loom three-quarters of a yard wide. This computation does not include the cloth made in private homes. The number of fulling machines or fulling mills is 1,630; carding machines run by water number 1,585; looms number over 330,000, weaving 75 million yards of material annually.

There are 207 gunpowder mills, producing 1,450,000 pounds annually. Paper mills and furnaces number 190 and 500, respectively. One would not be exaggerating to say that mills, particularly those for cotton and wool, have almost doubled since 1810.

AMDG[25]

Notes

1. Virgil, *Eclogue IV*.

2. In the United States, there are found more than twenty individual types of wild grapes.

3. A statement first attributed to King Henry IV of France and then popularized in America in 1928 by Herbert Hoover during the presidential elections.

4. The 1803 Louisiana Purchase was the acquisition of the extensive territory of Louisiana (about 827,000 square miles) that included land now part of fifteen present US states. This acquisition immediately doubled the size of the original United States.

5. In 1790 the US was principally a farming society aided especially in the South by the presence of African slaves.

6. James Monroe, 1817–25.

7. This was likely a misprint. In 1890 doubling the 1870 United States' estimate projected population should amount to 112 million, and the addition of a further half of the projected population's increase by the end of the century would make it a total of 173 million.

8. Established in the 1720s by Jesuit missionaries under the guidance of Father Joseph Greaton, an English Jesuit.

9. Fort Washington, completed in 1809, was then the only defensive structure protecting the United States' capital.

10. Originally called "Goose Creek," Tiber Creek was a small tributary to the Potomac River. In 1815 it was rerouted to become a part of the Washington City Canal. Later on, it was channeled underground.

11. A silver coin, the Spanish piece or Spanish dollar was also known as the piece of eight because at the time it was worth eight reales. Its minting and wide circulation began after 1598 as a match and rival of the German thaler.

12. From 1775 to 1785, George Washington (1732–99) was the supreme commander of the Continental Army; but after his election to the presidency, the command of the army was entrusted to Alexander Hamilton (1755–1804). During Washington's two-term presidency (1789–97), Hamilton served as secretary of the treasury (1789–95) and in the intervening years continued to lead a very active political life. In 1805 Aaron Burr (1756–1836), the vice president in the first term of Thomas Jefferson's presidency, accused Hamilton of having undermined his chances of being named again as vice president in Jefferson's second term and challenged him to a duel. Hamilton accepted, and the duel that resulted in his death was fought on July 11, 1804.

13. In the United States, by 1859 eighteen states had declared dueling illegal. However, the antidueling laws began to be strictly enforced only in the early years of the twentieth century.

14. The custom of apprenticeship came to America by way of England. When the term of apprenticeship was completed, former apprentices were free to earn wages as journeymen. When they accumulated enough money, they could set up a shop and join the appropriate guild pertaining to their craft.

15. An educational system promoted, among others, by Joseph Lancaster (1778–1838), an English schoolmaster who, in 1803, published an influential booklet titled *Improvements in Education*. His motto, "He who teaches, learns," induced him to experiment with monitorial teaching by more advanced students. This system was also adopted in some American schools, eventually leading to the rise of public education.

16. The word *as* refers to an ancient bronze roman coin that Roman students learned to subdivide.

17. Dr. Benjamin Rush (1745–1813), a signer of the Declaration of Independence and a father of American psychiatry, espoused the rather controversial and dangerous theory that a mental illness could be "shaken out" of mental patients.

18. Alexander Wilson (1766–1813), a Scottish American, is considered the greatest American ornithologist before Audubon.

19 John Chetwode Eustace (1762–1815), from an English family, was ordained a Catholic priest in 1813. His book on classical Italy met with great success. He died of malaria in Naples in 1815.

20. Antonio Canova (1757–1822) was the most important neoclassical sculptor. Perhaps, citing from memory, Father Grassi is confused, as Richmond's statue of General Washington was sculpted by the Frenchman Antoine Houdon. Instead, upon Jefferson's suggestion Canova's statue had been commissioned by North Carolinians for their state capitol. It was installed in Raleigh in 1821, and it was destroyed ten years later in an accidental fire.

21. Nathaniel Bowditch (1773–1838), an American-born mathematician and astronomer, became an extremely popular author with his works on navigation. His *The New American Practical Navigator*, first published in 1802, was inspired by the Englishman

John Hamilton Moore's less-than-perfect work *The Practical Navigator*. Robert Adrain (1775-1843), not "Adrian" as it appears in *Notizie*, was born in Ireland from a French father and a mother of Scottish descent. After the death of both his parents when he was only fifteen, he emigrated to America where he acquired a stellar reputation as a mathematician and original thinker. James Wallace, SJ (1787?-1850), an immigrant from Ireland and a promising science and mathematics scholar. Stilll a teenager on May 19, 1803, perhaps hoping for a degree of merit or patronage, he had written a very long letter to Thomas Jefferson expanding his thoughts on Thomas Paine's *Age of Reason* and its incompatibility with Saint Paul's thought on the celestial bodies, concluding that the Bible contains more philosophy than man in this life can pretend to. He joined the Georgetown faculty in 1805 at the age of only eighteen years. He stayed there until 1809, when he was called to teach at New York's Literary Institution. While in New York, in 1812 he published an influential scientific book titled *A New Treatise on the Use of the Globes, and Practical Astronomy or a Comprehensive View of the System of the World*. Upon the Literary Institution's disbanding in 1813, he rejoined Georgetown College, teaching mathematics, natural philosophy, and chemistry. In 1816, with Father Grassi's enthusiastic approval, he and his natural philosophy class performed an experiment in aerodynamics by launching from the college a gas-filled balloon that became the talk of the town. Coincidentally, he left Georgetown College in 1818, soon after Father Grassi's departure, having being sent as a missionary to South Carolina. In 1820 he joined the faculty of the South Carolina College, at Columbia, prompting his expulsion from the Jesuit order. He remained a priest all his life.

22. Actually, many other scientists contributed to the invention of the steam engine. However, Robert Fulton can be credited with perfecting it and, together with Robert R. Livingston, with building the first completely successful steamboat that carried passengers between New York and Albany.

23. In the 1822 Italian edition, this paragraph appears to have been misplaced on pages 54-55 rather than on page 53.

24. The first chaplain of the House was elected in 1789. A chaplain is elected at the beginning of each Congress for a term of two years. Some sixty chaplains of various religious denominations have served since inception.

25. AMDG is an acronym of a Latin motto attributed to Saint Ignatius of Loyola, and used by the Jesuits. It stands for "*Ad majorem Dei gloriam*" (for the greater glory of God). A second acronym OAMDG that is sometimes used, as Father Grassi does, at the very end of an entire work, stands for "*Omnia ad majorem Dei gloriam*" (all for the greater glory of God).

2

On the Various Sects
That Exist in the
United States

<hr/>

U PON ARRIVING IN AMERICA, an Italian is most struck by the state of religion there. Before beginning a discussion of this subject, I would like to present an article from the US Constitution regarding religion, which was added as an amendment:

> Congress shall make no law regarding the establishment of a religion, or prohibiting its free exercise thereof; or abridging the freedom of speech, or of the press; or of the right of the people peaceably to assemble, and to petition the Government for a redress of grievances.[1]

Therefore, in keeping with this fundamental law, every religion and sect is equally admitted and protected in America, unless its principles or the practice of them disrupt the civil order established by law. In other words, the government does not involve itself in religious affairs. The number of those openly contesting revealed religion is not as large as one might suppose, bearing in mind that that country is the refuge for every hapless European. The number of these people is restricted primarily to the French, who, if they do stop professing the religion of their fathers, never do so in order to join a Protestant sect. However, Catholics of truly exemplary and edifying conduct are not lacking among these same French. The indifference that is currently so predominant in Europe has a peculiar character in America. This does not consist of scorning or completely abandoning the practice of religion. On the contrary, religion is often spoken of, and generally with respect. It is as if God never manifested His precepts to man; nor pointed out the narrow path that leads to salvation and which is taken by few; nor warned of the wide and easy path taken by many, that starts out seemingly straight but inevitably leads to damnation. In other words, it is as if the Bible, which is widely read, highly esteemed, and regarded by all as the guiding precept of their religion, is not the infallible word of God. Every sect there is considered righteous and good, and every error committed by wretched mankind through weakness is considered insignificant. Following these principles, one should not be surprised that America is teeming with innumerable sects that subdivide and multiply every day. Although there are those who label themselves as being members of a certain sect, they might not profess attachment to the doctrine of the founders of that sect even though they continue to attend its congregations. They might label themselves as such just because they had been raised under that denomination. These people say they belong to a certain sect to show that they are not without religion, whatever may be their actual manner of thinking. Thus the modern Anglicans do not take into account their Thirty-Nine Articles, nor the Lutherans the Confession of Augsburg, nor the Presbyterians the teachings of Calvin and Knox; but they imitate their first preceptors, examining, changing, and deciding what seems best and most pleasing to them.

It must be noted that the word "sect" in America does not have the same meaning that etymology and our modern usage have given it in Europe. Thus it is very easy for them to say "I belong to this or that sect." Among the peculiarities of America commonly observed by writers is encountering people who have lived several years together without being aware of the religion of the other person. If they are questioned they do not respond saying "I believe . . . ," but only state "I was raised in such and such a sect or religion." *Liberality* is the motto that these sectarians constantly echo between themselves (rarely, however, in favor of the Catholics). Now they are abandoning not only their distinguishing principles but also the names of their sects. Their ministers preach that everything is the same, indifferent to the true and the false, the right and the wrong, the light and the darkness. In this manner, as one American writes, all the sects, already so persistent in their peculiar doctrines, are proceeding to form not a body (because there is neither head nor feet) but a chaos of every type of heresy, distinguished by the name *liberality*. Soon there will be only liberals and Catholics, both professing the truth to be one, but not being able to agree on error.

To illustrate better how religion is regarded there, I will present examples. In Georgetown, a suburb of the growing city of Washington, there was a regiment of soldiers who were obligated by regulation to attend church every Sunday. But, because the men belonged to various denominations, it was difficult to decide which church or congregation they were to attend. The predicament was diplomatically resolved as follows: on one Sunday they would go to the Catholic Church, on another Sunday to the Methodist, on the third to the Anglican, then to the Calvinist, and the like, starting the rotation over again when the first had ended.

It is not at all uncommon to encounter people who have professed all the sects, and it is interesting to hear the reasons for such changes. One woman figured that the best religion was the one whose followers were the most distinguished in the city. I do not know what sect she had been raised in, but having observed in front of the Congregational Church, the Sunday before, a greater number of carriages than elsewhere, she promptly became a Congregationalist. Her family changed residence, and she again changed her religion, to Anglican, on the principle of the carriages. When the family moved for a second time, she again changed her religion by the rule of the carriages. She finally married and embraced the religion of her husband, ready once again to change according to the carriages.

It is not rare to encounter parents who think it best not to inculcate their children with the principles of Christian religion, being content to raise them with natural honesty and leaving to the children themselves the eventual choice of the religion most acceptable to them. Sometimes one sees in the same family, therefore, as many different sects as there are family members. In New England the sects are stricter than elsewhere, yet various superstitions and vain observances are more in vogue there than in other areas, and the *stick doctors* find a better market there for their quackery.

The impartiality of the government in matters of religion, as is solemnly promised, is strictly observed. This was never more evident than in the following case, which occurred in 1813. The police of New York were searching for a thief who had committed a sizable robbery. The thief repented his misdeed and, while confessing his sin to Father Anthony Kohlmann, a Jesuit, he also handed over the stolen goods so the priest could make restitution to the rightful owner.[2] When that person received his goods from the priest, he called the police. The Protestant magistrate, upon learning the identity of the priest who performed the restitution, had Father Kohlmann brought before him immediately to ask him the name of the thief. The priest answered that he had this knowledge through the sacrament of confession, and he could in no way violate a secret that both natural law and the Catholic religion impose on confessors as most inviolable and sacred. The magistrate retorted that civil laws make no exceptions and, under severe penalty, command one who knows to divulge a criminal's identity. The priest responded in turn that he had every respect for the civil laws, but that they also guaranteed the free practice of the Catholic religion, which obliges the confessor to suffer even death before violating the confessional secret. The magistrate responded that this free practice was allowable only if it did not interfere with public welfare. The priest again answered that far from interfering, the Catholic religion greatly contributed to public welfare, rendering to everyone that which is his due. Out of this disagreement a formal lawsuit emerged, and Father Kohlmann made his appearance in front of the highest court of the city, accompanied by non-Catholic lawyers.

The trial began with the priest being asked the reasons for which he did not feel obligated to divulge the name of the thief, and these were briefly explained. Then Father Kohlmann's lawyers spoke, arguing excellently and compellingly in response to the prosecution's objections. They showed that Father Kohlmann could not be forced to identify the thief without an open violation of the laws of the state, which guarantee the free practice of every religion, not restricting in any way the practice of the Catholic religion, so ancient and widespread throughout the world, so recognized for its principles, so useful to the public welfare, all of which were demonstrated by the matter in hand. Before giving sentence, Dewitt Clinton, according to the practice of the English bar, gave a synopsis of what had been said.[3] Then, insisting on the spirit of the country's laws and on the principles of well-understood liberality, he concluded by saying that a Catholic priest could not justly be forced to make public crimes known only through means of confession, and that therefore Father Kohlmann was acquitted. This decision was applauded everywhere and was recorded as a precedent for similar cases should they occur in the future. The discourse of the lawyers and Clinton's, together with the circumstances of the trial, were published in a volume called the *Catholick Question in America*.[4] At the end of this volume is to be found a small treatise on the sacrament of confession that has proven very useful in strengthening Catholics on this point of faith, reducing prejudices and pointing out the errors of the Protestants against this salutary sacrament. Despite the indifference to the number of sects, there is much ostentation of piety, especially in the North, where everyone reads the Bible. In New England traveling on Sunday is not tolerated, even for couriers. Almost every year, various petitions are presented to Congress that would prohibit by law travel on the Lord's Day. The captain of the ship I sailed in from America to Europe would not allow the passengers to play dominoes or even to sing on Sunday. At the same time he made no fuss over the tremendous amount of cursing and swearing that issued from the mouths of the sailors. In fact, having reached port on a Sunday morning, he made them work the entire day without the least reason. The observance of holy days in the North was, in times past, excessively strict. There still exist in various states certain religious laws that insist on the observation of the Third Commandment, although they are no longer enforced. They are called "blue laws," and I will give a few examples here: "So that Sunday be strictly observed, those who wish to go to church would do well to saddle and bridle their horses the preceding day." "On feast days women will not be permitted to clean floors, make beds, or groom children...." "Beer is not to be made on Saturday, so that its fermentation does not labor on Sunday."

It is also worth observing that among this indifference and affected liberality, Protestant ministers often inveigh against the Catholic religion, with which they do not know how to make peace. The prejudices brought two centuries ago from England are still pronounced in America, where one often hears those old slanders that are recognized as false even by honest Protestants. Thus, last year a Methodist publicly stated, "You ask me if it is permissible to go to the churches of the other sects: yes, be liberal, by all means go to the Anglican, the Quaker, or the Anabaptist church, but never, never go to the Catholic church, because they worship a *wooden God.*" Last June, another minister in Philadelphia concluded a fiery declamation against the Catholics with these words: "This impious, idolatrous, sacrilegious church deserves, and must be, destroyed."

I must, however, render justice to the Protestant people who disapprove highly of these transports that are so illiberal. If the bitterness of these ministers remains unrestrained, it is due to the laws of the present government. In the past, the situation was in a much worse state, as can be seen from the *blue*, or penal, laws, of which I add other examples: "Any person convicted of witchcraft will be hung, or closed in a sack and thrown into the sea...." "Quakers (much less Catholics) will not be permitted to reside in this state (in New England), and if one is discovered he will be executed...." "Anyone convicted of having sheltered a Quaker will be fined 40 pounds sterling for the first offence; for a second offense he will have his tongue perforated by a red-hot iron and will be banished; if he returns he will be executed." I have been assured that before 1776 in Virginia there existed a law (now abolished) to shoot any Catholic priest caught there, and that the state of Massachusetts accorded freedom to every Christian religion except the only true religion, the Catholic Church, and to the Jews.

From the arbitrary interpretation of Sacred Scripture, there often results truly lamentable effects, and many innocent people, despite all their goodwill, are befuddled by every doctrinal wind that comes along. In Southington, Connecticut, there are some that observe Saturday and not Sunday as the Sabbath, citing God's command in the Bible.⁵ In Pennsylvania there is a sect called the Hamony [*sic*] Society, which is headed by a leader who explains the Bible to the members. A few years ago, having read in Saint Paul that virginity is better than marriage, he promulgated an order that everyone should observe chastity. Many furious objections were made that *melius est nubere quam uri* [it is better to marry than to burn with passion, 1 Cor 7:9] but to no avail—the old man was inflexible. Although no one celebrated matrimony, there were still fathers, mothers, and newly born.... The old man protested vehemently, and they let him do so. Finally, he had to discontinue his crazy demands because a revolt was about to explode that threatened to put an end to the colony and to his authority. In the spring of 1812, in Virginia, a well-known preacher revealed, both through the printed word and from the pulpit the fatal prediction that the end of the world would occur that July 4th. The people believed him and let the season pass without planting or cultivating their land, saying, "Why do we have to work if the world will end before the harvest?" I could cite many other examples, but I will omit them for the sake of brevity.

It would be a truly difficult undertaking to enumerate the various sects into which the inhabitants of the United States are divided. Moreover, it would be impossible to give an exact account of their beliefs and opinions. I will try, however, to mention something of them by presenting briefly the current state of these sects. I will leave to the good sense of the reader to make the many conclusions that present themselves herein. The principal sects of America can be reduced to the following: Congregationalists, Methodists, Anglicans, Presbyterians, Anabaptists, Universalists, Unitarians, Lutherans, Quakers, Dunkers or Mennonites, and Craistians.[6] To give an idea of each one, I mention that which is peculiar to them, having found few people in Italy who are knowledgeable about them.

THE CONGREGATIONALISTS

Beginning from the northern states, the most numerous sect to be found there is that of the Congregationalists. These do not really form a group unified by doctrine, nor do they have a leader. Instead, each congregation or parish is independent, and it lays down or alters its own credo as it sees fit, and only those who wish to partake of the so-called *Lord's Supper* are obligated to subscribe to this credo. The manner in which the first ministers of this sect were ordained was very peculiar, and thus it deserves to be mentioned here. The first Congregationalists were Anglicans who came from England to settle at Plymouth and Salem in Massachusetts. Since no minister came with them, Endicott, the governor, wishing to remedy such a disadvantageous condition, convened a large meeting, during which he proposed that some ministers should be ordained.[7] Everyone consented, and a day of fasting and prayer was declared. Afterward, nominations were made, and several of the most respectable members of the colony were designated as the ordainers. On the day set aside for ordination, the *elders* performed the laying on of hands, along with other rites used on similar occasions by Anglicans. After this was done, each person came forward to offer the new preachers the *hand of fellowship*.

In Newhaven a certain Mather did not approve of that manner of ordination and proposed something better.[8] He gave a long sermon on the text *Sapientia aedificavit sibi domum, excidit columnas septem* (Prov 1: Wisdom has built her house. She has erected its seven pillars). Then he said that seven men must be selected, to whom would be left all the details and handling of the ordination, and thus it was done. The validity of these ordinations was attacked violently by the Anglicans, but the Congregationalists did not become disheartened, and to uphold them they imitated the first early reformers of the sixteenth century, and by making a small alteration in the English version of the third verse of chapter 6 of the Acts of the Apostles they claimed to refute the Anglicans. They made a new edition of the Bible, and where the Latin text reads *quos constituamus super hoc opus* (whom we appoint this task; Acts 6:3) they wrote *quos constituatis* (whom you appoint), and by substituting a *you* to a *we*, believed to have settled the whole matter. But the alteration was discovered, and the Anglicans condemned that Bible, declaring that they would not avail themselves of any other scripture but the Anglican one.

To give some idea of their beliefs, which change according to what suits them, I will make mention of the Congregationalists of the Saybrook Platform, who undertook the formation of their own credo.[9] They adopted the symbol of the Apostles, which had been rejected by others, and they decided that, in case of diversity of opinions concerning biblical meaning, the only rule of their belief was to have recourse to the Greek or Hebrew text, which no one or very few knew. As time passed, it became evident that their credo was not faring well, so they created another, which had a rather short duration. But the credo of the Apostles was always rejected, in the modest belief that it was the Apostles, and not they, who were in error.

The Methodists

In about 1730 two Anglican preachers did with their church what their fathers had done without reason with the Catholic Church. Whitfield and Wesley separated from the Anglican Church, which they criticized openly as being fallen from its original purity, infected with error, and lacking in the spirit of God.[10] The enthusiasm with which they preached won them many followers, particularly among the common people. As their lives were very methodical, these people came to be called Methodists. They kept many articles of the Anglican Church and also taught that true Christians were animated by the Spirit of God, who inspires and directs them to obey His bidding. Finally, they taught that deeds considered sinful by others were meritorious for Methodists, and they regarded themselves as the holy chosen ones, the only true Christians. They often talk of spirit, therefore, and attribute to it every type of oracle. The Methodist is convinced that he is in the grace of God, but why? Because the Spirit assures him of it. He says he will never go astray because the spirit gives him this assurance. It is impossible for him to suffer damnation because the Spirit promises him eternal salvation. Often, when meeting each other, they ask,

"How is the spirit?" They sing hymns at the bedside of their sick to rein-vigorate the spirit. They display much fellowship among themselves while disdaining all others, regarding them as unclean and sinful. This sect ad-mits a type of public confession. Not long ago, during an assembly, a per-son confessed to having had illicit intercourse with a woman, naming this other guilty person, who was then present along with her parents.

No one is considered a true Methodist until he has made proselytes, and these are not admitted among the *holy* people until they have been converted. This conversion is very strange, and some learned people even believe that occasionally some malevolent, invisible entity intervenes. The man or woman (there are considerably more women than men among the Methodists) to be converted is led near the pulpit, on which the minister, wrapped in a black cloak, preaches and often screams, like a madman. All the most terrible aspects of a depiction of hell, demons, and Judgment are pronounced with a thundering voice. With great emphasis and in an un-restrained shout, he invokes Christ: "*Here He is,*" he screams, "*Here He is, you see that He has come.*" The Methodist bystanders cry out, repeating the minister's words, "*Here He is, here He is,*" while some raise their arms or kneel, others prostrate themselves, and some fall to the floor. The preacher then comes down from the pulpit and, kneeling, continues to speak to Christ as if He were present, beseeching Him for the conversion of those present. A mixture of moans, shrieks, and cries resounds on every side. If, during all this, the new Methodist falls to the ground, they say the con-version has been performed. Then the mood completely changes: there is much applause, many hurrahs, shouts of joy rise up everywhere, and tri-umphant hymns are sung with fanatical enthusiasm. All this usually takes place at night, and many attend these assemblies as if they were spectacles of amusement.

Because these sects are hardly known on the continent of Europe but are making rapid progress in England and the United States, I would like to elaborate on the assemblies that they call *class-meetings* and *camp-meetings.* *Class-meetings* are assemblies in which men and women shut themselves in a room and sometimes confess to each other. *Camp-meetings* are held once a year. Toward the end of July, an announcement is published in the gazettes of the date and location of the camp meeting and of the name of the minister who will direct it. The locations usually are in large forests far from settled areas. The Methodists go there in large covered wagons furnished with enough food and provisions to last fifteen or twenty days.

The number of these wagons—containing men, women, children, and Negroes—is, at times, so large that one might mistake it for an army's baggage train. The principal function of the *camp-meeting* is preaching, and to do this it is not necessary to have been ordained. A cobbler, tailor, or a Negro—who may or may not be able to read the Bible—preaches and screams with all the power of his lungs, making his squawking heard from a distance of miles. After the preaching, the listeners divide up into smaller groups, each in the form of a circle. He or she who has most need of venting the agitating spirit goes to the center and prays in a loud voice while making strange movements with the arms, eyes, and lips, continuing in this way until the point of exhaustion. Then another replaces the first and carries on the same scene, until yet another steps in. To justify their screaming, they usually quote what Saint Paul says of Jesus Christ: *In diebus carnis suae preces supplicationesque cum clamore valido offerens* (In the days of His flesh He offered prayers and supplications with vehement cries; Heb 2). The person they call the sergeant regulates the sale of beverages and food and maintains order. The shadows of the forest and the darkness of the night create circumstances that in themselves are easily imaginable, but about which I prefer not to write. I only add that as a consequence of the moral disorders taking place at these assemblies, the legislature of Kentucky passed measures prohibiting these *camp-meetings* in that state, according to articles in the gazettes of 1816. The things that the Methodists denounce most often, and with great fervor, are playing cards, fancy clothing, frequenting taverns, theaters and race tracks, cock fighting, and other things of a similar nature, which truly are very far removed from the spirit of Christianity.

Soon after this sect was formed, it divided in two. Some followed Whitfield, while others followed Wesley, and new divisions take place rather frequently. Many have abandoned this sect because they have discovered much hypocrisy in it. I have seen in print the following dialogue between a shopkeeper and his servant, both Methodists: "William, did you put sand in the mascabà?"[11] "Yes, sir." "Did you add water to the liquor?" "Yes, sir." "Did you wet the tobacco well?" "Yes, sir." "Then come on up and we will say prayers."

One could never finish recounting the eccentricities of the preachers of this sect. In offering another example, I repeat what was told to me by a credible person. A minister in the pulpit observed that while the offerings were being collected, a man was trying to decide which small coin he was going to donate. The minister pointed to him, shouting: "*There is the demon of avarice tempting that sinner; but you must resist the temptation and donate your large coins instead of your small ones.*" Another concluded his sermon as follows: "*I beseech you, oh Lord, to convert as many as you can, and the ones you can't convert, crush with your fist so that they fall in pieces to roast on the burning coals of hell. Amen.*"

THE ANGLICANS, OR EPISCOPALIANS

Because the United States were British colonies until the year 1776, it is not surprising that they abound with Anglicans. The king of England, who is head of that church, fostered its development in America, even making donations of land that have grown to considerable value in our day. It is known that the Anglican beliefs are contained in the Thirty-Nine Articles, some of which were found incompatible with the new system of government established at the time of the American Revolution. For this reason, Anglican ministers convened to adapt their articles of faith to the new circumstances. The first article to be cancelled was that concerning the primacy of the king, for which so many Catholics have suffered the most barbaric treatment. Then they rejected the first four councils as well as the three symbols, those of the Apostles, the Nicene, and of Saint Athanasius, the latter particularly because "of his damning clauses," which state that those who do not profess the Catholic faith will be damned. The representation of the English bishops notwithstanding, the American Anglicans favored the symbol of the Apostles, justifying their decision in a most peculiar tract. Examining the articles with Bible in hand, they decided that *descendit ad inferos* was not very clear, so they cancelled it. The Anglican liturgy was greatly altered under the pretext of purging it of some remaining influences of papism. These innovations displeased many, and many refused to conform. Another assembly was therefore convened in which the old liturgy was reinstated and, in regard to *descendit ad inferos*, the matter was left to individual discretion to accept the translation "he descended into hell" (with which many were scandalized) or its alternative, "he descended into the region of the dead."

In order to cut all political and religious ties with England, a certain Seabury traveled to England to be ordained a bishop in order that he could ordain in his turn upon his return to America.[12] But the Anglican bishop, accustomed as he was to receiving a sizable payment from every ordainee, and learning of Seabury's unwillingness to disburse, refused to ordain him under the pretext that he wished to obtain the permission of the king, head of the so-called Anglican Church. However, Seabury presented himself to unsworn bishops in Scotland by whom he was favorably received, and he was ordained by Bishop Skinner.[13] After this, the English bishops created no further difficulties in ordaining Americans. Thus Madison, White, and Provoost—all from the United States—were ordained in England, and upon their return they established their alleged hierarchy independent of the English. A certain Davis suggested that it would be good to have an archbishop in America, but this proposition was rejected because it smacked of papism, and the public would be displeased with such a title and dignity of office. The other Protestant sects have much to say against Anglicans because they call themselves antonomastically "the Church," not showing thereby the liberality practiced by the others, and because they are convinced that they are the only ones following the straight path of truth. I must point out here that Anglican ordinations have never been recognized by the Catholic Church.

THE PURITANS

In America Puritans are commonly called Presbyterians, because they allow priests but not bishops. Originally, they followed the teachings of Calvin and Knox, but today they are far from swearing on the word of those teachers. Their doctrine on predestination is the teaching that others find hardest to accept, and their own preachers are unable to agree among themselves on this point: if one is chosen, he will be saved no matter how bad his deeds; if one is not chosen, he will be damned despite all the good he has done. Prejudice against Catholics is perhaps stronger and more radical in this sect than in any other. The ordinations of the Presbyterians are considered worthless by the Anglican Church, and every Puritan minister who goes over to the Anglicans must be reordained, not *sub conditione*, but absolutely. The Presbyterians are divided into two large bodies, which in Scotland are called "burghers" and "antiburghers." A general union of the dissenters was attempted, but it did not succeed. But some united and thus formed a third sect, known as the Associated Reformed Presbyterian Church.

THE ANABAPTISTS

A certain Rogers was the first to introduce the errors of this sect in America, preaching the uselessness of infant baptism and the necessity of baptism by immersion for adults.[14] Because of this new doctrine he was exiled, and he and his followers were forced to withdraw to Rhode Island. This sect is already divided in two: one group is called the "open communion" because they allow anyone to partake; the other is called the "strict communion" because they adhere strictly to the original doctrine of the sect, allowing only members to partake of their mysteries and regarding all others as unclean, and unworthy, prevaricators.

THE UNITARIANS

Joseph Priestley, the Englishman so renowned for his knowledge of chemistry, turned at one point to theology.[15] On the principle that one should not believe that which is not within reach of one's understanding, he rejected the ineffable mystery of the Holy Trinity, which is infinitely superior to the myopia of human reason, and recognized but one divine person. The followers of this doctrine were called Unitarians. Originally, this sect did not make so rapid progress as it is now making in the United States, especially because a certain Freeman began preaching in Boston.[16] To gain more authority he wished to be ordained, but the Anglican bishop Seabury refused to ordain one who would spread such an impious doctrine. Freeman was not dismayed; he mounted the pulpit and, telling of his rejection, added, "What need is there to be ordained by an Anglican? Have not you, my dear congregation, equal power to ordain me? Yes, and for myself I would be extremely satisfied to be ordained by you." This proposal was accepted, and the ceremony was performed in the manner described when I spoke of the Congregationalists. And, lo and behold, here was the ordained Freeman, who then himself ordained others, who scattered here and there to disseminate the doctrine. The sect already has many converts, and it has found the means to build a large meeting house in Baltimore, not far from the Catholic cathedral.

THE UNIVERSALISTS

The founders of this new sect taught that at the resurrection, on the day of final judgment, all men will be saved, and that the souls separated from bodies remain in a state of total inactivity, like snakes in the winter. But toward the end of the last century a certain Winchester, of the state of Massachusetts, corrected this.[17] He taught that after death, sinners will be punished severely, and that they will be admitted to eternal glory only when they have been purged and cleansed of every blemish of guilt. At the same time he rejected the Catholic doctrine of Purgatory. He also taught the concept of universal restoration, that all men in the end will be restored to the state of original justice and happiness from which they fell through the sin of our progenitors. Because of this doctrine, the Universalists are sometimes called Restorationists.

THE QUAKERS

The Quakers' origins, character, and beliefs are well known, but many are not aware that it is already divided in two: the Friends and the Shakers. The former have deviated considerably from the simplicity affected by their forebears, and today they enjoy the luxury of carriages, expensive furniture, silver, and fine clothes tailored, however, in the Quaker manner. Their air of simplicity notwithstanding, they are extremely shrewd in the pursuit of their own interest and, therefore, some of them are very wealthy. But far from growing, their number seems to be decreasing considerably. Years ago, Philadelphia was considered a Quaker city, but today one sees no more of them there than in any other large American city.

The Shakers reside principally in the state of New York. To account for this name, some say that one of the original Quakers, brought to trial in London, seriously spoke to the judge as follows: "If you do anything against the Quakers, be aware that I will make you shake," and hence the name "Shakers." According to others, they received this name because in their congregations, they begin to tremble or shake from head to foot. They say that the reason for such a strange practice comes from the announcement of Saint Paul: *Cum timore et tremore operamini salutem vestram* (Work out your salvation with fear and trembling; Phil 2:12–13).

Besides the shaking, the men still dance separate from the women. They dance in silence until they are tired, or until someone moved by the

Spirit begins to preach, whereupon everyone listens intently. This sect has one religious community for men and another for the women. He who enters must renounce matrimony and remain celibate.

THE DUNKERS

This name denotes a small number of sectarians in the state of Pennsylvania. They usually wear beards in the manner of Polish Jews, and this is their most distinguishing feature. I must admit that I never came to know the beliefs that they profess, but only, so I was told, that they are frequently employed in the fields as overseers of Negroes. Some confuse them with the followers of the Swedish Swedenborg, who is well known for his knowledge of mineralogy and even more so for his dreams or self-proclaimed visions of a new Jerusalem.[18] Thus this sect is called the New Jerusalem. In other places in the North, there are Brethren of Moravia and other sects whose origins are described in the modern dictionaries of heresies. But as the sects continually change, these books are unable to define them properly.

THE CHRAYSTIANS, OR CRAISTIANS

The Chraystians, or Craistians, are sectarians who have recently arisen in New England. They assume the name of Craistians—that is, Christians—because they claim to imitate the example of Christ more closely than any other group. Their conduct resembles strongly that of the Methodists. They reject the glorious mystery of the Holy Trinity and claim to be enlightened directly and at once by the Holy Spirit. Contrary to the custom of other Protestants, they do not make use of the Bible. Rather, they say, they could create another Bible that would be better than the existing one. They usually hold their meetings in the fields and in the woods, and anyone can act as leader or minister in their practices without regard for sex or age. Some women even have become traveling preachers, and they have been seen entirely alone, without provisions, preaching on a circuit of hundreds of miles. At least these women maintain a certain decorum in their ministries, but the men behave in the most excessive manner: they gnash their teeth, engage in fist-fighting, carry arms, contort their mouths and make all sorts of strange faces, and sometimes explode into uproarious laughter, apparently without the slightest reason. Sometimes they direct their discourses at individuals, particularly those who seem most inattentive to their sermon, scolding and insulting in the rudest of terms and accusing of incorrigible sinning. They have introduced the use of the public confession, and the most nefarious baseness does not restrain them from their impudent disclosures in front of scandalized bystanders.

Finally, I mention a certain Jemima Wilkinson, who believed herself to be, and passed herself off as, the chosen woman of the Apocalypse, and who created a lot of commotion, though attracting few followers.[19] She is now living a quiet life at her New York retreat.

Those are the seven principal sects in the United States. Something must be said also of the manner in which persons are admitted to their communion. It is a common sentiment of the sectarians that before being admitted, each person must have been chosen and called internally to the state of grace. The sign of this calling is a great alarm, an internal fright felt by the chosen one. One found in this state is said to be in anxiety. This lasts for some time, occasionally months and years, while the person's thoughts center on the danger of their damnation, the severity of divine justice, the anger of the offended Omnipotent, and other terrible subjects. They appear dejected, with pallid and sad faces, and this anxiety has been known to end in madness, desperation, and even suicide.

Then arrives the great moment for many of them, when they emerge from the darkness to experience the most brilliant and dazzling light (if one is to believe their accounts). They not only rise up out of the state of desolation, but they also claim that they receive the infallible certainty of heavenly glory or, as they say, confirmed faith. Then they ask for communion with the Lord. An assembly is held in the church for those who are to receive communion, and each petitioner goes forward to give the proof of the experiences he has undergone. If his account is satisfactory, he is accepted as a candidate. For several days church officials gather much detailed information on the candidate, some of which is not completely modest or without wickedness. Finally, the candidate is allowed to receive communion. In order to avoid such a long process, others wait until an awakening to petition to receive communion. The *awakening* is a period of time during which an extraordinary fervor is aroused in the sect, or in the congregation, such as might occur in the time of a public calamity, or after a fiery sermon delivered by a new preacher. On these occasions it is easy to receive communion, but afterward many remain unaffected by the experience.

I seek here to add to the reader's knowledge of the current state of American sects, although one must remember that there are many exceptions. Most sects today make use of excommunication, which usually means deprivation of communion or exclusion from entering the church or taking part in assemblies. These reprisals are taken against those who too strongly oppose the articles of the sect or who comport themselves in a scandalous manner. The sentence is pronounced by a majority of votes of the leaders of the congregation (among the Anglicans, it is decided by the minister), and it must be confirmed by the bishop. It is then announced at a public meeting, and, if the offender is present, he is led outside the doors of the church by two deacons. Such cases are, however, rare.

The various congregations select the preacher who suits them best. These preachers, despite declaring their alleged devotion to the faith they represent by saying *I am an Anglican, a Methodist, a Calvinist*, and the like, are asked all the same to deliver a sermon, in order that their personal views may surface as well as to demonstrate their eloquence. This obsession with hearing eloquent sermons is very widespread in America; some foreigners have been known to remark that religion there has almost been reduced to the desire to hear preachers of beautiful words. Thus the principal study of ministers is preaching, and they emphasize elegant speech that flatters and entices the ear. Their sermons are frequently discourses by honest men rather than Christian teachings. Sometimes they are political dissertations according to the party that is most popular among the congregation. The preachers affect indifference, speciously calling it liberality toward other sects, but they command their followers not to stray from their faith.

If the Catholic Church is seldom the object of their liberality, the reason can be easily understood by those familiar with this religion. In truth, it seems strange that honest and often judicious and learned men maintain such gross prejudices and palpable errors against Catholics. One is less surprised, however, if one goes beyond the merely educational factors and observes that the circumstances of Protestants in America are very different from those of Protestants in Germany and England. In Europe the very walls of their temples, the inscriptions on the graves of their fathers, the sacred furnishings of their churches, the many monuments that still exist, and readily available books all inform the Protestant of his deviation from the religion of his fathers, and it seems to him as if his schism has been thrust in front of his face. But in America there are none of these signs; everything is new, and in many areas nothing has been heard for over two centuries but the repetition of the same prejudices and insults against Catholics carried down from their ancestors. Some have never seen a catechism or even heard a Catholic preacher. In fact, many who have embraced the faith have ingenuously confessed that they had never suspected that they were in error.

Switching from sect to sect, or even to Catholicism, is an everyday occurrence, though it entails much sacrifice, and it is rarely done except in the belief that it is best for one's personal salvation. I was told that several ministers, after considering the invalidity of the ordinations of their sect, quickly abandoned it to embrace another, which, they believed, had a regular succession of pastors invested with the authority that had been passed down from hand to hand from Christ Himself. This is what three Congregationalist ministers did. They were professors at the college of New Haven; one was named Brown, another Johnson, and the third name I do not recall. The famous Anglican bishop Berkeley (the one who in defending the spirituality of the human soul went so far as to negate the existence of the body) had brought with him to America a large library of books, which he donated to the abovementioned college before returning to England.[20] Among these books were works by the Holy Fathers, and the three abovementioned professors began to avidly read those volumes so rare in America. From this study they learned of the nature and the necessity of true ordinations, and that those not performed by the legitimate successors of the Apostles cannot be true. A little reflection convinced them that the Congregationalist ordinations were not authentic. After conferring among themselves, they decided to leave their honorable and lucrative positions and so became Anglicans, whose ordinations they erroneously believed to be valid; however far they are from being recognized by the Catholic Church.

I have mentioned this only for the sake of describing the disposition of many sectarians in America, and to show that there is merit in the opinion of those who believe that many of the sectarians' errors are only material in nature. In fact, many of them do not have the slightest difficulty in attending a Catholic service. An Anglican minister cordially invited Monsignor Cheverus, the bishop of Boston, to sing a Solemn Mass in his Anglican church.[21] A black minister of African Methodists in New York repeatedly asked the Jesuit Father Anthony Kohlmann to preach in his church, but Kohlmann declined. There are excellent books of polemics in the English language, but until recently they have only enjoyed a very limited circulation. I doubt if there is a complete collection of the works by the Holy Fathers, which, if there were, many would consult with much enjoyment and profit.

The Catholic doctrine of the unity of the true Church of God appears to many as being too severe, but, because it is so concordant with common sense, it has made a considerable impression on serious-minded people. But alas, there are so few of them that are such! How many ministers demonstrate apathy toward the religion with which they were raised, caring only for the temporal remuneration that is presented to them? It is certain that many are negligent in attending to their most important functions, and for this reason the Catholic bishops had to order the rebaptism *sub conditione* of each sectarian who embraces the Faith. Six years ago, an Anglican minister in Maryland substituted cider for wine during the communion ceremony, and the fraud was discovered. After being rebuked by the authorities, he coldly responded "that wine was scarce and everything is the same." In other places, because of their ignorance or deviousness, communion is celebrated with gooseberry wine. They print *religious tracts*, which are pamphlets that contain religious teachings and exhortations to lead moral lives. These are distributed without charge to their followers, but every precaution is taken so that they do not fall into the hands of Catholic priests, who would point out the contradictions and errors and the insubstantiality of their principles. These ministers are not able to combine the doctrine they teach with the sentiment of the pretended liberality that they profess. Among them stands out one who candidly confessed that the Catholic religion was the true one, although he had four objections against it. *Which ones?* He was asked. His response: *three children and a wife to support.*

One circumstance that should not be omitted is the facility with which a minister may leave or reenter the ministry, passing from one type of life to another that is totally different. Thus a certain Anglican deacon named Kilbourne left the ecclesiastical profession and became a land speculator.[22] He moved further inland, and there he started to preach again, winning the approval of the people. Then he was made a justice of the peace but left this position for the more lucrative job of land surveying. The knowledge of the land that he gained earned him the job of postmaster, which he then quit on accepting the rank of major in the militia. He later was elected to the state legislature, and finally he became a member of Congress in

Washington. Examples like this are rather common, and they illustrate well what I have asserted above.

Elsewhere, I have alluded to how some consider the multiplicity of sects as being the disastrous seed of future discord or an undetected flame that will suddenly explode into ruinous fire. They say that if now one does not see the dreadful effects, it is for the same reason that the fatal consequences of dissension with regard to political matters are not more considerably felt. What will become—continue these observers—of a state where there is no deep-seated unity of spirit or harmony? And could this unity ever come about when there is so much discrepancy between opinions, systems, and religious beliefs? If the difference between one sect and another consists only in the variety of rites, clothing, or language, then one should have no reason to fear the effects resulting from these differences. But it is common that one sect regards another as inimical, as abhorrent, as an entity that prostitutes itself, and so on. As for those who believe in following the impulses of that which they call the Spirit of God, one must ask to what excesses will this lead without heeding another guide?

The influence of this sectarian spirit is becoming more evident every day. In some parts of New England, the Congregationalists behave as if their sect had been given the position of dominance by civil law. The deans of a college in New York have been known to exclude from their number anyone who did not belong to their sect. This influence is also clearly demonstrated in the distribution of certain jobs, in the opposition of one sect to another, and in the pressuring used to influence another to convert to one's own sect. They conclude that as it becomes more difficult to prevent or impede these circumstances vis-à-vis the present system, the effects will be all the more serious and harmful.

Will silence be imposed? But the sectarians will object, citing the Constitution, which guarantees freedom of the press and speech. Will learned men be authorized to decide controversies? But who would ever accept the decisions of men who confess their fallibility, and have no greater right than anyone else? This sort of submission would be a tyranny unknown even to papism; while if the Catholic Church demands submission to its doctrine of faith, it also teaches that it is supported by the spirit of truth promised it by Jesus Christ, and thus that it is infallible. Should it be mandated that each person remain with the same faith that he began with? But the sectarians would object, saying that their spirit cannot approve this, for our ancestors were ignorant and lived in the dark ages, while the American sectarians have been enlightened, and, if this rule were instituted, then everyone would be led back to papism. Will the government take the authority to decide? But this is against the Constitution, and if civil laws become the rule of our faith, then one who travels to England must become Anglican; to Russia, Greek Orthodox; to Constantinople, Turk; or to China and Japan, idolatrous. Common sense would not support such a measure. It would be a mockery of God and man.

But let us put aside these conjectures that others are making regarding the probable results of an ever-growing number of sects that enjoy such unrestrained liberty. This pertains to the future, and I have said that I would speak of the present circumstances. It would not be out of place, however, to mention here an important question that has been proposed by others. Everyone is inclined to pity and to treat with appropriate charity one who has been raised in ignorance of the truth, or one who is unable to recognize it when it is properly revealed to him. But this unrestricted liberty to preach every sort of error, to even offend God, is another matter, one that deserves serious attention. Because of it, doctrines are being spread that degrade man to the level of a brute beast, and, besides being injurious to our celestial Father, this unsound policy will have serious effects on the state.

To conclude this portion of the book dealing with the current sects in the United States, I present lists of the various religious organizations in New York. These provide a picture of the state of religion in that city that one can proportionally apply to other cities of the Union:

Number of various churches existing in New York

6   Dutch Reformed
6   Puritan
5   Methodist
2   Negroes Methodist
1   German Reformed
1   Evangelical Lutheran
1   Jewish synagogue
1   Moravian Brothers

1   Associated Puritan
1   Puritan Associated with the Reformation
1   Reformed Puritan
5   Anabaptist
11   Anglican
There are two Catholic Churches: Saint Peter and Saint Patrick.

Other associations
Biblical Society of New York
Auxiliary Biblical Society of New York
Auxiliary Bible and Prayer Book Society
Women's Biblical Society
Union Biblical Society
Society of the Religious Tracts, for the free distribution of religious
    publications
Anglican Society of the Tracts
Society to Provide the Gospel to the Poor
Missionary Society
Junior Missionary Society Evangelical Society
American Biblical Society
Unitary Society for Sunday Schools
Young Missionary Society
Young Society of the Tracts
Society to Promote Industriousness among the Poor
Society to Suppress Licentious Habits
Women's Society of Lidia
Women's Society for the Assistance of Widows with Family
Women's Society of the Cent (every member sets aside a penny each day
    for the poor)
Aid Society for Mutual Help
Aid Society
Society for the Relief of Needy Old Women
Society to Support Widows of Anglican Ministers
Polish Society of Charity for the Jews
2 Women's Association for Maintaining Charity Schools
Anglican School of Charity
Anglican Society to Promote Religion and Instruction in the State of
    New York

Dorcas Society
Society for the Protection of Orphans
The Freemasons have 20 public lodges.

AMDG

NOTES

1. First Amendment to the US Constitution. Its ratification was completed on December 15, 1791.

2. Father Anthony Kohlmann, SJ (1771–1836). Born in Alsace, then a French territory, in 1803 he became a Jesuit in Russia, a country that had ignored the suppression of the order. He then was sent to the United States, first to Georgetown, then to New York, to be sent again to Georgetown, where, in 1817, he was named superior, as well as serving from 1817 to 1820 as president of Georgetown College.

3. The mayor of New York, Dewitt Clinton (1769–1828), as well as the city's district attorney, Barent Gardenier (1776–1822), decided to rule in favor of Father Kohlmann, thus setting a very important juridical precedent.

4. The volume was written by William Sampson (1764–1836) and was published in New York in 1813 by Edward Gillespy. Sampson was the Irish Protestant lawyer who defended Father Kohlmann and was a strenuous champion of religious and civil liberties both in Ireland and America.

5. Both the Old Testament and the New Testament refer numerous times to the observance of the Sabbath—for instance, Genesis 2:2–3; Exodus 20:8–11 and 31:16; Leviticus 23:3; Hebrews 4:1–16; Deuteronomy 5:12–15; Isaiah 58:13–14; Ezekiel 20:12–24; Matthew 24:20 and 28:1; Luke 4:16 and 23:56; Colossians 2:16–17; Acts 1:12, 13:42, and 17:2; and Mark 2:27–28 and 16:1.

6. Interestingly, the Lutherans that Father Grassi places among the principal sects of America that he plans to discuss are nowhere to be found in the pages that follow.

7. John Endicott—or Endecott—(1588–1665) was a magistrate, soldier, and first governor of the Massachusetts Bay Colony, which subsequently became the Commonwealth of Massachusetts.

8. Increase Mather (1639–1723) was an influential Puritan minister who was involved with the government of the Massachusetts Bay Colony and was the father of Cotton Mather. Consistently with the Bible's teachings, that *Sapientia aedificavit sibi domum, excidit columnas septem* ("Wisdom has built her house and hewn out seven pillars" Proverbs 9:1), seven men whose judgment can be relied on were chosen to handle the ordinations. See also Acts 6:3: "Brothers and sisters, choose seven men from among you who are known to be full of the Spirit and wisdom. We will turn this responsibility to them."

9. Preceded by the Cambridge Platform (1648), the Saybrook Platform (1708) was yet another attempt at reining in the autonomy of the individual congregations by

making them subscribe to a more centralized system, similar to that adopted by the Presbyterians.

10. George Whitfield (1714–70) and John Wesley (1703–91), with the help of Wesley's brother Charles (1707–88), all of them Anglican ministers, in about 1738 began an evangelical revival that, in 1795, four years after John Wesley's death, culminated in a schism from the Church of England. While agreeing on most doctrinal points, George Whitfield and John Wesley differed in their interpretation of the concept of predestination, with Whitfield believing in preordained divine salvation or damnation, while John Wesley trusted in God's unconditioned universal love for all and in the sanctifying power of the Holy Spirit.

11. From the Spanish *mascabado*—a word referring to minimally refined sugarcane, used mainly in baked goods.

12. Samuel Seabury (1729–96) was the first American Episcopal bishop and an English loyalist.

13. In 1783 Samuel Seabury had been elected bishop at a meeting of Anglican clergy; however, he could not be consecrated because in America there were no Anglican bishops there, so he left for England to be consecrated. In London the Anglican bishop refused to consecrate him, saying that, because he was an American citizen, he could not take the oath of allegiance to the king. Seabury then turned to the Scottish Episcopal Church and went to Aberdeen, where in 1784 he was consecrated by Bishop John Skinner (1744–1816) and two other bishops, Robert Kilgour and Arthur Petrie, who by so doing can be credited with transmitting to America the apostolic succession.

14. By Rogers Fr. Grassi meant to refer to Roger Williams (1605?–83), a former minister of the Church of England who became a Puritan minister and a Reformed Baptist theologian, migrating to the New World in 1630, where he founded the Colony of Rhode Island and the Providence Plantation. He held radically egalitarian beliefs for the times, such as religious freedom, the separation of church and state, liberty of conscience, the abolition of slavery, and the fair treatment of American natives.

15. Joseph Priestley (1733–1804)—an experimental chemist, a multifaceted scholar and philosopher, the author of more than one hundred and fifty publications, and a preacher—was born in England in a dissenting, non-Anglican family. In 1760 he joined Unitarianism, an antitrinitarian religious movement that preached that God was a single being and that Christ was only a divulger of God's truth. Politically of liberal convictions, in some writings he endorsed both the French and the American revolutions, but an enraged mob burned down his home and the Unitarian church where he preached. No longer willing to live in England in 1794, he migrated to the United States.

16. James Freeman (1759–1835) was minister of King's Chapel in Boston for forty-three years and advanced greatly the Unitarian cause.

17. Elhanan Winchester (1751–97), a Baptist minister, upon reading a book titled *The Everlasting God*, written under the pseudonym of Georg Paul Siegvolck by the

German author Georg Klein-Nicola, converted to Universalism. The Saur Bible, the first German Bible printed in America, was influenced by Elhanan Winchester's belief in universal salvation.

18. Emanuel Swedenborg (1688–1772)—an influential scientist, philosopher, and Christian mystic and theologian—inspired his American followers to create the Swedenborgian Church in North America. However, more likely, the Dunkers' distant origins may be traced to the teachings of John Wycliffe and John Hus, and mainly to central European early Reform movements. Now known as Church of the Brethren, its early name derives from the baptismal practice of full immersion.

19. Jemima Wilkinson (1752–1819)—and not "Wilson," as Father Grassi wrote, probably from memory. Born to Quaker parents, she was the first self-styled American prophetess, declaring to her numerous followers that she had died and been sent back from Heaven as neither male nor female. She had started her ministry in 1776 in Rhode Island, after a vision she called "The Publick Universal Friend" began inhabiting her body. A strong captivating personality, she preached the Ten Commandments and sexual abstinence, eventually leading her followers to an inhabited area of central New York State, where they founded Jerusalem Township, on the west side of Seneca Lake.

20. George Berkeley (1685–1753)—but in Grassi's book he appears cited as Berkley—was an Anglo-Irish Anglican bishop and a philosopher and writer who came to America. His dream of building a divinity school was not realized during his lifetime, but in 1733, when he went back to Europe, he left his real estate and considerable theological library to the young Yale College, in New Haven, Connecticut. Samuel Seabury, the first American Episcopal bishop, was a Yale College alumnus. The present divinity school, created in 1854, is named after George Berkeley and has preserved its Anglican origins.

21. Jean-Louis Lefèbvre de Cheverus (1768–1836). Born in France to an aristocratic family, and ordained a priest, in 1792 he escaped the hostile climate of the French Revolution by repairing in England. In 1796 he traveled to Boston and joined the Indian Mission in Maine, distinguishing himself during the 1798 outbreak of yellow fever. In 1810 he was created a bishop of the newly created Boston Diocese. In 1823 he returned to France, where he served as bishop of Montauban and, in 1826, was promoted archbishop of Bordeaux. In 1836 he was created a cardinal, dying soon after.

22. James Kilbourne (1770–1850), cited in the book as Kilburn, was a land surveyor from Ohio and an Episcopal clergyman. He was elected a member of the US House of Representatives for Ohio's Fifth District, serving from March 4, 1813, to March 3, 1817. Here, too, Father Grassi, citing some English names, seems to have adopted an approximate Italian form of phonetic spelling and pronunciation.

3

On the Present Condition
of the Catholic Religion
in the United States

————⋙•⋘————

T HE CATHOLIC RELIGION is more widespread and well regarded in
America than many may suppose. However uncouth and ignorant a person may be, he would willingly acknowledge that the
Catholic Church is the earliest of all; and many non-Catholics prefer to
communicate their religious doubts to a Catholic, simply because he pro-
fesses the faith which is the first and oldest. Our missionaries are generally
respected, either because of their education and superior knowledge, or
for their celibacy, for their unselfish and zealous labors, or, ultimately, because of the undoubted validity of their ordination. It is a noteworthy fact
that when the impious Thomas Paine was on his deathbed, he gave strict
orders that no Catholic minister be admitted to his room; but he allowed
the Catholic missionaries, then two Jesuit priests, to be called, who came
and spoke with him. It seems that now and then he paid some attention to
the truths that they suggested to him, but the acute pains that tormented
him caused him to break out in horrid curses and shudders of despair. The
fathers, having failed to accomplish anything, withdrew in horror, and he
died as unbelieving as he had lived. Paine was an Englishman who had
been a corset maker before he became a writer and philosopher on religion. His principal work, *The Age of Reason*, is remarkable if only for the
unbridled vehemence with which it speaks against revelation.[1]

The Jesuits, who propagated the Catholic faith in Canada, and spread
it so extensively throughout South America, were also the first missionaries in the territories that now form the United States. No less than two

hundred English Catholic families, who had been bitterly persecuted for their faith in their native land by their fellow countrymen who proclaimed themselves to be the apostles of liberty of conscience, immigrated to Maryland in 1633 under the auspices of Lord Baltimore. Father White, a Jesuit, along with some other members of the Society, accompanied the first settlers, and from then on the colony continued to be a Jesuit mission of the English Province.[2]

Because my objective is to speak only of the present state of affairs, I will not describe here how those good Catholics, by an unprecedented display of generosity, so vaunted in our times and so little practiced by their adversaries, gave asylum to non-Catholics in the colony they had founded, and how they were repaid with ingratitude by those whom they had befriended, and were cruelly persecuted by the English government. I might add, however, that the Jesuit missionaries, even after the suppression of the Society, continued to develop those missions, and to found new ones, under the jurisdiction of the vicar apostolic of London.

The number of Catholics having greatly increased, the See of Baltimore was established by His Holiness, Pius VI, and the Reverend John Carroll was appointed its first bishop, to whom a coadjutor was assigned in the person of the Monsignor Leonard Neale.[3] They were both ex-Jesuits and natives of Maryland. Bishop Carroll was consecrated in 1790 at Lulworth Castle, the residence of Thomas Weld, one of the principal Catholics of England, who lived an exemplary life and died a true Christian. The consecrating bishop was Monsignor Walmesley (that same one who, under the name of Pastorini, had published the history of the Christian Church taken from the Apocalypse).[4] The bishoprics of Boston, New York, Philadelphia, Bardstown, and New Orleans were subsequently founded; and in 1810, Bishop Carroll was advanced to the position and title of metropolitan archbishop. It seemed truly to be a sign of divine providence that this dignity was bestowed on one whose character was best qualified to dispel prejudices against the Catholic Church, and to familiarize that part of the new world with a correct idea of it. Monsignor Carroll, a native of that country, enjoyed all the educational advantages which the Society of Jesuits provides for its members. He was professor of theology at the College of Liège, and, before 1773, he had been admitted to the profession of the four vows.[5] He had accompanied Sir Gage and other English noblemen on a tour through Germany, Italy, and France, and everywhere

he had made the most favorable impression. Nor could it have been otherwise, because, along with his irreproachable conduct, he possessed a profound knowledge of Catholic doctrine, and his accomplished manners and
kindness of heart were accompanied by rare prudence. He thus won the
affection and respect of Catholics and non-Catholics alike. Among others
who honored the archbishop of Baltimore with their friendship was the
glorious hero of America, the immortal Washington.

Having reached the age of eighty, Monsignor Carroll passed from
the world to a better life in the spirit of strong Christian fortitude and
edifying interior peace. His death occurred on the Feast of Saint Francis
Xavier in 1815. The day of his funeral was a sort of triumph for the Catholic
religion, as the ceremony was conducted with all the pomp that would ac-
company such an occasion in an entirely Catholic city. His mortal remains
were placed in the sepulcher of the Sulpician Seminary, until the completion of the cathedral, when they will be deposited there, according to his
wishes. This was the first time that Baltimore had witnessed the rites of a
Catholic burial service in full accordance with the ritual: the cross borne
at the head of the mournful procession, the priest chanting in sorrowful
strains, the funeral trappings, the burning candles and the expressive
ceremonies made a deep impression upon the people who, in respectful
silence and with signs of mourning, professed affection and esteem for the
good prelate whom they had lost. The Catholic Church of America will
always have the glory of having begun its hierarchy in a new land with
such a worthy and meritorious man as Monsignor Carroll. His successor,
Monsignor Neale, soon followed him to the grave, in June 1817; his memory will be honored particularly in those places where he worked so hard
to advance the spirit of piety.

In 1820, two new bishoprics were established, one in Charleston, South
Carolina, and the other in Richmond, the capital of Virginia. This brings
the number of bishops in the United States to nine. The other seven are in
Baltimore (an archbishopric); Philadelphia; New York; Boston; Bardstown,
Kentucky; New Orleans; and Cincinnati. In Europe the title "bishop" im-
plies greatness, even in the secular world; but in America these prelates, to
the great edification of all, are constantly engaged in those tasks and labors
of simple missionaries. Imagine my surprise in 1810 upon seeing the archbishop of Baltimore and metropolitan of the United States enter a house
along with me, and then, having drawn from his pocket a wide ribbon to

serve as a stole, place upon a small table the holy oils, a vial of water, and a little ritual for the baptism of a baby. The same is done by the other bishops in their respective dioceses, and Monsignor Flaget of Kentucky made the visitation of his diocese traveling alone hundreds of miles on horseback.[6] I should point out that the names "congregation" and "missionary" are equivalent to "parish" and "parish priest." I shall say nothing with regard to the number of Catholics scattered throughout the vast expanse of the United States, as there are no reliable statistics on this, but it is relevant to mention something briefly with regard to each diocese, beginning with the North.

THE DIOCESE OF BOSTON

Catholic missionaries are stationed in only two places in the Diocese of Boston, at Boston and on the Penobscot River in Maine. The Abbé Matignon, a Frenchman, has succeeded in founding a church in the capital of Massachusetts,[7] and Monsignor Cheverus, also a Frenchman, presently resides there.[8] The amiable character and the conspicuous virtue and learning of this prelate and his worthy assistant have won the respect and esteem not merely of Catholics but also of those who are outside the realm of the Church: all have been inspired with the highest ideals of our religion by the lives of such excellent ministers. The Penobscot missionary works with a tribe of Indians who have not yet forgotten the Jesuits, from whom they received the message of the Gospel.[9] Throughout the rest of New England, Catholics are very few, and there are no missionaries.

THE DIOCESE OF NEW YORK

The number of Catholics in the city of New York is reputed to exceed twenty thousand, most being Irish, with a remarkable commitment to the faith. The new Church of Saint Patrick, which is Gothic in style, is considered to be one of the finest buildings in the United States, and serves as the cathedral of Monsignor Connolly, an Irish Dominican.[10] He is assisted by only two missionaries, both of whom are advanced in years. One can imagine how great their labors are in a city of such size. At Albany, the state capital, there are a church and a missionary, who also administers to the Catholics living at considerable distances. In almost every village of this state there are good Irishmen, always ready to contribute to the building of churches and the support of missionaries, if they could obtain them.

THE DIOCESE OF PHILADELPHIA

The Jesuits from Maryland built the first church in Philadelphia, Saint Joseph's, which together with the adjoining residence still belongs to them. There are three other churches here: Saint Mary's, under the direction of the bishop; Holy Trinity, which is mainly attended by the Germans; and Saint Augustine's, erected through the efforts of Father Carr, an Irish Augustinian.[11] There are altogether five priests in the city who also visit outside missions. Even before that of Philadelphia, the Jesuits had founded other missions in Pennsylvania. One is at Conewago, where four fathers of the Society reside. This and the neighboring congregations are made up of German settlers, who still preserve their commitment to the ancient faith as well as their simple German customs. Another mission is in Lancaster, and the missionary residing there also has charge of six other congregations, each one needing a priest. To avoid entering into trifling details, I merely mention that in 1813 there were in the whole of this extensive diocese no more than thirteen priests, among whom Prince Demetrius Gallitzin, a Russian, deserves special mention for the zeal with which he carries out his missionary duties.[12]

THE DIOCESE OF BARDSTOWN, KENTUCKY

The most remote areas of this diocese were formerly considered an extension of Canada, and for that reason many inhabitants of those parts are French; moreover, many families also have immigrated to that area from Maryland in search of better land, leaving behind land that had been worn out by the long, continuous cultivation of tobacco. The present bishop resides in Bardstown, where he maintains a little seminary and has begun to build a church to serve as a cathedral. In 1813, there were only eight priests in the whole of this vast diocese. The missions are perhaps more laborious than elsewhere, because the Catholic population there is more scattered and poorer. In the neighboring territory of Illinois, there are various Indian tribes, some of which were brought to the faith by the Jesuits long ago; but for the most part they still live in total ignorance of the true God.

THE DIOCESE OF BALTIMORE

The Diocese of Baltimore once comprised all the southern and southwestern localities of Maryland. There are five churches in Baltimore, including the cathedral, which is still unfinished. It is being built of the hardest granite, from the designs of Latrobe, the chief government architect.[13] The church of the Seminary of Saint Sulpice is Gothic but elegant. Because Maryland was a Catholic colony, the missions are more numerous there than in any other state. In the new city of Washington there is a large congregation but only one priest, who officiates at Saint Patrick's Church near to which the Jesuits have built a house designed for the education of youth. Some years ago, the foundations of a cathedral were laid, but the construction had to be suspended for lack of funds. In Georgetown, besides two small chapels there is the Church of the Holy Trinity, which unfortunately is not large enough to contain more than a third of the people who flock to it. This church is served by the Jesuits residing at the college.

In Maryland the Jesuits have four residences, and other missions, each serving several congregations. In 1813 there were about forty missionaries in Maryland, a number utterly inadequate to administer to the needs of the Catholic population. An individual missionary must therefore compensate as much as possible for the lack of laborers. Some idea of the journeys and fatigue of such a life may be gathered from the annexed list of places administered to and visited in 1817, by one priest. Father Malevè, SJ.[14] He resided in the town of Frederick, where the congregation is fairly numerous. Besides this, he had to go to the Manor, a distance of 7 miles; Maryland Creek, 15; Hagerstown, 28; Martinsburg, 38; Winchester, 50; and Cumberland, 110. These places have large congregations and spacious churches. To these we must add four smaller congregations and various scattered families, which this one priest must visit occasionally.

The cities of Norfolk, Portsmouth, and Alexandria in Virginia have Catholic churches. Richmond, Petersburg, and Fredericksburg have made efforts to obtain a priest, but without success, and for this reason there are as yet no churches in these places. Charleston, South Carolina, as well as Augusta, the capital of Georgia, and Savannah, Georgia, each have one church, and missionaries reside at distances of over one hundred miles from each other. By now, even Fayetteville and New Bern, North Carolina, have this advantage.

A report on the accomplishments of Monsignor Dubourg, the bishop of Louisiana, has been published in Paris and Turin.[15] Thus I consider it redundant to repeat here in my limited account what is contained in those pages. From this brief description, one can see the great need there is for priests in America. Moreover, the settlers that move from the coast further inland are most anxious to have churches and priests; many landholders, even Protestants, offer hundreds of acres gratis for this purpose, not through any special zeal for religion but simply as a matter of speculation. Indeed, people always prefer to settle in places where they can easily procure the assistance of religion, and consequently the lands increase in value. Missionaries who would establish themselves in such places would have the consolation of seeing the whole neighborhood embrace the Catholic faith. But where, where can so many zealous priests be found today?

For those wanting to know who are the ones that toil in that large vineyard of the Lord, I briefly mention the religious clergy to be found there in addition to the secular clergy. The Jesuit fathers, besides their missions, have at Georgetown, near the rising city of Washington, a pleasantly situated boarding college, which was authorized by an act of Congress on March 1, 1815, to confer such academic honors as are customary in the other colleges or universities of the country. The Jesuits also directed a school in New York, called the Literary Institution; it has been closed, solely for lack of teachers, but they still possess the property. The Sulpicians have a creditable college at Baltimore, chartered as a university by the Maryland Legislature. In addition to the Seminary at Baltimore, they also maintain a school at Emmitsburg.[16] The English Dominicans have in Kentucky a convent and school, and the Church of Saint Rose of Lima, and in 1816, besides some novices, they had four students of theology. There are only three priests, who are in charge of a few missions, and four or five students. They have a great need there for liturgical books, and they are forced to remedy this situation by their edifying activities.

Despite their small number, these priests have already been able to begin the founding of a new mission in the state of Ohio. Monsignor Fenwick and Father Young have offered themselves for this undertaking, on which our Father has bestowed His ample blessings.[17] In September 1821, one of them wrote to his brother, a student at the Jesuit seminary in Rome, that upon their arrival, the vicinity of their place of residence had only eight or ten Catholic families; but in the space of three years, there were more than two hundred, the majority having been converted from the various sects of that country. Father Fenwick continues to labor as a simple missionary, even though he has recently been appointed bishop of Cincinnati, one of the most prominent cities of that state. He still administers to the thirty posts that he has established there. He was fortunate to have the consolation of a very favorable assistance from Europe.

Another Dominican, the Englishman Father Hill, embarked at Leghorn in the spring of 1821 for America, along with other priests of his order. It is already known that this excellent priest has safely arrived at his destination. Those places that would be fortunate to have a missionary of such merit would indeed be delighted. Several lay missionaries have also journeyed from Italy to the Western territories of the United States. Their superior was the commendable Mr. de Andreis from Piedmont, who soon won the affection and esteem of all who came to know him.[18] Although he had inspired the expectation and hope of great forthcoming benefits in those areas, our Lord had other plans for this invaluable missionary, and he passed on to a better life to enjoy the rewards of his apostolic labors.

In America there are also some communities of religious women, the oldest of which is the Convent of the Discalced Carmelites of Saint Theresa. Three nuns of this order had the courage to leave their English convent in Antwerp and cross the wide Atlantic to found a new house of their order in Maryland; in a few years their number had increased to twenty-six, and their convent, an entirely wooden structure, is not far from Port Tobacco.[19] Archbishop Neale, filled with zeal for the education of youth, has established at Georgetown a community of Visitation Nuns for the Christian education of girls. In a short time this community has increased so rapidly that presently it numbers seventy nuns.[20] Another institution for the same purpose has been founded at Emmitsburg by the Abbé Dubois; the teachers and sisters have adopted and follow, as far as circumstances permit, the rule of the Sisters of Charity, who in France are principally occupied with service in hospitals.[21] Some of them have moved from Emmitsburg to Philadelphia, where they have been entrusted with the care of an orphanage. On feast days they lead the orphans in procession to the various churches, to the admiration and edification of the public, and to the advantage of the benevolent institution, which is supported by the alms of Catholics and even good-willed Protestants. These same sisters are now even established in Baltimore, where they are involved in the education of poor girls and run an orphanage. In Kentucky the Abbé Nerinckx, a most zealous priest, has founded a congregation called the Daughters of Mary at the Foot of the Cross.[22] Finally, Abbé Thayer, a Calvinist preacher who became a Catholic at Rome, and who died not long ago in Ireland, has left funds sufficient to found in Boston, his city of birth, a house of Ursulines for the education of young girls.[23] This has now been opened, and it has four nuns and several novices.

CHURCHES AND FUNCTIONS

The churches are very simple buildings without ornamentation, often with internal galleries to provide more space. The organ, if they have one, is located above the main entrance, and they have only one altar. Behind, or alongside the altar, there is a small sacristy, in which confessions are heard, and it is furnished with a fireplace. Mr. Peemans, the Countess De Wolf, and Father Geerts, formerly a Jesuit, and other benefactors from Flanders, with a generosity equal to their zeal, have sent to America many decent and even beautiful vestments, which were much needed and of which there is still a great deficiency. One cannot describe the good effect that religious paintings have on the people. The few paintings they have represent a well-known mystery in the life of Jesus Christ. The most common is the Crucifixion, in front of which people are moved to tears, particularly the unlearned ones, and even sometimes Protestants. But, unfortunately, paintings are rare, and of little artistic merit, being the work of non-Catholic artists. I make particular mention of this circumstance to confirm the observation made by many, that non-Catholic painters do not succeed in imparting to their works that air of piety that so much inspires devotion. The most remarkable church in North America, in terms of structural magnificence and ornamentation, is surely the cathedral of Baltimore. It is 190 feet long, including the front portico; and the transept is 77 feet wide. The diameter of the dome is 66 feet, and it is 116 feet above the floor. In the two wings and at the end of the church, there are five galleries: one for the organ, which is the most considerable in those territories; one for the young people who are still unmarried; one for the children of the schools of charity; one for Negro men; and one for Negro women.

Besides the main altar, there are two lateral altars; the first is of solid marble, and it was donated to Monsignor Ambrose Maréchal, the current archbishop, by several ecclesiastics in Provence who were students of his.[24]

Next to this altar are two statues of angels in the attitude of adoration. Another altar will be erected toward the end of the cathedral, *a cornu epistolae* (facing the altar), and this will serve particularly for the sacrament of Holy Matrimony. A baptistry of marble will be placed in front of this altar.

The cathedral is adorned with several good paintings; two were donated by the Most Christian King (Louis XVIII of France), and eight were donated by His Eminence Joseph Cardinal Fesch.[25]

Above the two sacristies there are two large rooms in which the present archbishop intends to establish a library for his clergy. From America, he writes, "I would be happy if I could gather a certain number of good books that lay useless and worm-eaten in the numerous libraries of France and Italy." The cost of the cathedral's construction amounted to about 1 million francs. There is, however, a debt of 200,000 francs, but one hopes that the generous faithful of both the old and the new worlds will contribute enough to satisfy this debt.

I shall say nothing of the services in city churches, because they are the same as in Europe, so far as the number of priests will permit. But it will not be without interest to describe those that are held in country churches located far from towns and residences, which are by far the most numerous. On Saturday, the missionary leaves his residence and travels to lodge with some Catholic living near the church. Having arrived at the house, he puts the Blessed Sacrament in a fitting place, along with the Holy Oils, which he always carries with him on his travels. On the following morning he rides to the church and ties his horse to a bush. The whole morning is spent hearing confessions. In the meantime, people from distances of four, six, and ten miles, and even more, arrive on horseback, so that often the church is entirely surrounded with horses. Mass begins around noon; during the celebration, those who can read make use of prayer books, and pious hymns, for the most part in English, are sung by a choir of men and women. The Gospel, read in the vernacular, precedes the sermon, while the entire congregation remains standing out of reverence. The preacher either reads or recites his sermon, according to his inclination, and sometimes it is deferred until after Mass, to enable the priest to take some refreshment, which the faithful never fail to provide. There is no necessity to command attention, because they display the greatest eagerness to listen to the word of God. Vespers are not said, as the people live so far off and are so scattered; so, when Mass is over, the children recite the catechism and infants are baptized, or the customary ceremonies are administered

to those who are already baptized. Prayers for the dead are recited, or funeral services are offered for those who have been buried in the church-
yard during the priest's absence. Finally, the priest must attend to those
who ask for instruction in order to join the Church, or who wish to be
united in the bonds of Holy Matrimony.

Having finished all these tasks, the missionary remounts his horse and
goes to dine at a neighboring house; invitations are not wanting. On fes-
tival days, especially, he is informed of grave cases of sickness; these sick
calls are the most laborious work for the missions, both because of the long
distances and their frequency. Sometimes those good people show a lack
of discretion by summoning the priest even when there is no danger.

A Dominican father on one occasion traveled thirty miles through
woods in order to assist a sick woman; imagine his surprise to find her
well enough to mount a horse and act as his guide to point out the way
back, the return trip being another thirty miles! On these visits, it is often
necessary to begin by giving conditional baptism to the sick, for they cannot tell whether they have already been baptized or not; the negligence
of non-Catholics on this specific point is very great. Cases frequently occur of those who have never been Catholics but who wish at least to die
within the bosom of the Church. They know nothing, and there is no time
to impart any teaching, or they are incapable of comprehending it. On
such occasions, one must be satisfied with getting them to make acts of
theological virtue and helping them understand as much as possible those
truths that are necessary for salvation. This is true especially in the case of
Negroes, with a *Credo quidquid Catholica credit Ecclesia* (I believe whatever
the Catholic Church believes).

All these functions must at times be performed in private houses for
the convenience of families too far removed from the church; the order
observed is the same as that described above. If one would ask how these
churches are built and maintained, I would answer that generally they are
maintained by the voluntary contributions of the faithful, who donate a
certain amount for the building. When the church is built, those who want
a seat reserved for their exclusive use pay a nominal amount, which helps
to support the church and pastor; but this is not the case in some Jesuit
missions. This is customary especially in the cities and villages. Indeed,
in some places, the pews in the church are sold to private families, and
one such sale, in 1815 in Saint Patrick's Church of New York, produced
the sum of $37,000. The so-called Incorporated Clergymen of Maryland

hold lands by virtue of an act of legislature.²⁶ These lands could be made to yield considerable revenues if they were properly cultivated, but the means are lacking to accomplish this. It must be noted that every bequest for religious purposes must be made in the name of an individual, as the laws of the country are opposed to bequests of the type that could be made in Italy.

The situation of a missionary in the United States will be better understood if I briefly mention the special difficulties as well as rewards he encounters in exercising this ministry. I do not consider learning the English language to be difficult, for in the space of about six months one can attain proficiency sufficient to hear confessions and give public instruction; nor does one need to contend with indifference to religion, for this evil is less common there than elsewhere. The civil laws, which permit complete liberty, cannot be considered troublesome. One of the greatest difficulties to be encountered, however, and which needs only to be experienced to be understood fully, is that one is left completely alone, and sometimes at a distance of twenty, fifty, one hundred miles, or more from any other priest. Moreover, because Catholics live so far apart, one must labor a great deal to gather even a little fruit; hence, if new and inexperienced missionaries are not careful in the beginning, they run the risk of ruining their health. Considerable difficulties arise from cases in which non-Catholic slave masters who are bitter enemies of the faith deny their slaves the permission required by law to contract marriages and the like.²⁷ These complex cases of conscience have hardly been dealt with in books by otherwise knowledgeable authors. Mixed marriages cause great embarrassment and trouble; sometimes the husband hinders his wife from receiving the sacraments, or the wife does not allow the children to be brought up in the faith.

This reminds me of an odd incident that happened to Father Francis Neale while baptizing a little boy in the house of a Catholic gentleman. In the middle of the ceremonies, the Protestant mother rushed into the room in a fury, snatched the child from its godmother's arms, and carried it off, declaring that no child of hers would ever be baptized by a priest. It should be noted that such a title is not used for sectarian ministers, but only for Catholic priests. There are cases of couples marrying before non-Catholic ministers because they do not research the couples' bloodlines and care little about their spiritual dispositions. Such an act is regarded as an act of apostasy, and those who are guilty of it are not permitted to receive the sacraments until they have performed public penance. What afflicts the good missionary priest most grievously is the evil conduct of some Catholics, whose lives are in contradiction to the sanctity of the faith they profess, and who are the greatest obstacle to the conversion of others. How painful it is to hear those who have traveled in Catholic countries speak of the lax observance of holy days, the unedifying conduct of the clergy, and the lack of devotion in the churches there, and then to see these Catholics, rejected from Europe, come to America and perpetrate the greatest scandals against religion. This is much more grievous than the poverty that at times afflicts the missionary, who is barely supplied with the necessities of life and is without the means to establish a school, to decorate the altar, and to help the indigent sick.

In the midst of such difficulties, God is very generous in granting many consolations to sustain His servants. It is no small matter that as in the past, in America one can still say with heartfelt gratitude that at least the Catholic religion is not persecuted by public authority and enjoys peace. The labors of some missionaries are not constant, and they may have entire weeks to rest, or to devote to prayer and study, provided that sickness is not prevalent. If they are grieved at seeing some neglect their Christian duties, this grief is often compensated for by the pleasure of encountering excellent families, especially in rural districts, who, although they see the priest only once or twice a year, lead eminently Christian lives and strictly observe the prescribed fasts, recite their prayers in common, unite together on Sundays for spiritual readings, and say the prayers for Mass as if they were actually present at the Holy Sacrifice. They see some who journey over a hundred miles to fulfill their Easter duties, bringing their grown-up children for baptism and instruction, and carrying back a handful of consecrated earth to cast upon the graves of their dead.

What can I say of the happiness one feels upon witnessing the signs of divine providence, when children after baptism, or adults shortly after their conversion or after being fortified by the sacraments, die sweetly in the peace of the Lord? What can I say of the triumphs of grace in certain remarkable conversions? Two years ago, at least three Protestant ministers embraced the faith, thus renewing the edifying example set in former times by Lord and Lady Warner, who after abjuring their errors and having provided for their children, entered religious orders by mutual consent. Many examples of remarkable conversions might be mentioned here, but for brevity's sake I limit myself to two. A distinguished Quaker woman, a so-called spiritual master of her sect, upon hearing that there were Catholic priests in New York and that they were Jesuits, was fired with zeal, and resolved to go and convert those whom prejudice had her believe to be the worst abomination of the antichrist. She soon found them and immediately launched into such a virulent diatribe that one of the missionaries thought it best to leave the room. The other, an American, better acquainted with the customs of his country, listened to her with patience. He replied with politeness and did not lose his temper when interrupted, and thus calmed down her fury somewhat, and rendered her docile and attentive to his discourse. God blessed this conversation, and others that were held upon the subject of religion, and having abandoned her false notions, she finally recognized the truth and embraced it.

The other example is of a young Methodist preacher named Richard, who likewise went to convert the priests of Saint Sulpice in the College and Seminary at Montreal in Canada. His undertaking had excited the highest expectations among the members of his denomination; but imagine their amazement, and the satisfaction of Catholics, when it became known that Monsignor Richard had been converted to the faith, and afterward became a priest, and finally professor of theology, an office he continues to execute with honor to the present day.

I must not omit the very great consolation that Negroes bring to the missionary. Although they are poor slaves and thus abject in the eyes of the world, some of them are chosen souls filled with such beautiful sentiments of true piety that they move one to tears, and the missionary himself is further encouraged to work for the glory of God. The frequent offering of their labors to the Lord, their patient endurance of ill treatment from unprincipled masters, their obedience for the love of God, and the recitation of the rosary when possible are the devotions chiefly recommended to them, and which they for the most part practice; consequently, Catholic slaves are preferred to all others because they are more docile and obedient to their masters.

There is reason to believe that the situation of missionaries will become less arduous in the future, because in addition to the fair number of excellent young American men who have already entered the religious vocation, many priests have already left for America to share the labors with those already there. Up to the present time, there were not enough priests even to administer to the Catholics, and they were practically unable to provide instruction to those who wished to enter the Church and to the Indians who are still in ignorance of the true God. A letter written recently from Washington reports that some Indian chiefs, who had recently called to pay their respects to President Monroe, paid a visit to the neighboring Georgetown College. Upon seeing the Jesuit fathers, these Indians manifested their joy in the most touching manner. They said that they had often heard their fathers speak of the Black Gowns, and they offered every inducement to persuade them to return with them to the forest, promising that their tribes would heed no other prophet or teacher except the Jesuits. Poor people! Since the suppression of the Society, they have been deprived of all spiritual assistance.

The truth can be proclaimed freely and be triumphant in America because there it does not need to contend with one of its primary obstacles—namely, civil authority—which hinders truth elsewhere and in our day seems inclined to favor irreligion and error. Furthermore, in America there are attitudes more naturally inclined to piety and devotion, and religion will make rapid progress if it is proposed with the gentle charity that characterizes the true ministers of Jesus Christ. A person acquainted with ecclesiastical history is startled upon hearing the names of certain sects and shudders to recall the wild doctrines held by their founders and the bloody excesses that marked their founders and their origin. But matters are quite different in our day. Many individuals, it is true, bear the name of those sectarians, but they are far removed from the primitive spirit of their sects. They are gentle in character, upright in their lives, polite in their manners (there this virtue, however, is more or less common also to those who are not Christians) toward all types of people, whatever may be their real inner beliefs. After having conversed with many of them, and having heard their admiration for the apostolic courage of the reigning pope and their ridicule of those who even today consider the pope to be the antichrist, one is then quite surprised to hear that he has been speaking with a Quaker, a Methodist, or a Puritan. Conversely, there are Protestants in whose minds the mere mention of the words "Roman Catholic" conjures up horrid pictures of the many atrocities maliciously charged to the Catholic Church, which their preachers paint in vivid colors: the horrors of the Night of Saint Bartholomew, the Gunpowder Plot, the Great Fire of London, the abuses of the Inquisition—such detestable principles as, for example, that one must not keep one's word given to heretics; and that priests give license to misbehave to those who perpetrate the blackest crimes by promising to absolve them if they share in the spoils of a crime, such as theft. These errors not only are not taught but are abhorred and explicitly condemned by every Catholic; they are time-worn insults, often acknowledged to be such by honest sectarians but still daily repeated as unquestioned facts in conversation, in sermons, and in printed books. Hence, it is no wonder that the name "Catholic" is equivalent to "monster" in the minds of many Protestants, for the prejudices of early education are deeply rooted. But if the genuine principles of the Church with regard to doctrine and morals are explained to them in a gentle manner, with patient and kindhearted charity, and especially if they become acquainted with a well-educated Catholic of irreproachable life, they are incredulous and exclaim with amazement: "Is that the teaching of the Catholic Church? That upright gentleman is a Catholic? How different it is from the idea I had formed of it!"

I must conclude this subject here, because the copious and interesting material of this topic has led me beyond the limits of my intended brevity. How many more observations might be made here upon the vicissitudes of empires and nations, the arts and sciences, the proclaimed right of interpreting the sacred Scriptures to suit individual caprice! How many reflections might be made on the benefits that can be expected from Bible societies, which degrade the Bible in front of people of every class and walks of life, placing in everyone's hands the most sacred gift that mankind has received from God, changing the truth into a source of error and death! How many reflections might be made upon contradictory liberality of those who present the Bible as the only rule of faith, and at the same time legally impose a belief dictated by men who acknowledge themselves to be fallible, and who change the articles of belief to suit their whim and pleasure! How many of these reflections, which will readily appear in the minds of all good Christians, will induce them to pray to the Author of our Faith for the prosperity of the Church in America, and to contribute some offering for the benefit of the missions and the decoration of their churches!

I will not dwell upon these reflections, because they will be obvious at once to the impartial reader of these pages; and besides, the sole object I had in view was to make known the current condition of the Catholic Church in the United States of North America.

OAMDG

Notes

1. Thomas Paine (1737–1809). His most important work, *The Age of Reason: Being an Investigation of True and Fabulous Teaching*, written probably during his stay in France, was issued in three parts. The first part, published in 1794, came out almost simultaneously both in French and English editions. The second part was first published in a pirated edition (London: H. D. Symonds) and then, in 1796, by Eaton, which published it together with the first part. The third part, dealing with controversial biblical exegesis, and in spite of being ready for publication as early as 1802, fearing possible reprisals, was published only in 1807 in America, where in 1774 Paine had fled from France.

2. Andrew White, SJ (1579–1656), an English Jesuit, was a cofounder and the chronicler of the establishment of the Maryland Colony.

3. John Carroll (1735–1815), who was ordained a bishop in England, was the first American Catholic bishop and the first archbishop of Baltimore. He was instrumental in reorganizing and in firmly establishing the American Catholic Church. Leonard Neale, SJ (1746–1817), was ordained a bishop by John Carroll, becoming the first Catholic bishop ordained in America. From 1799 to 1806, he served as president of Georgetown College.

4. Charles Walmesley (1722–97), a Benedictine monk, was titular bishop of Rama and the vicar apostolic of England's Western District. Under the pseudonym Signor Pastorini, he published the controversial, but very popular among English Catholics, *General History of the Christian Church from Her Birth to Her Triumphant States in Heaven Chiefly Deduced from the Apocalypse of St. John the Apostle*, in which he prophesized the demise of Protestantism by 1825 and in particular the destruction of the Anglican Church.

5. The year 1773 was when the Society of Jesus was suppressed by Pope Clement XIV. A few years earlier, some European Catholic states, uneasy with the powerful order, which had aroused some antagonism also within the papal curia, had ordered its expulsion from their countries: Portugal, in 1759; France, in 1754; Spain, in 1767; and the Austrian Empire, in 1770. The society was reconstituted some forty years later by Pope Pius VII after the fall of Napoleon Bonaparte in 1814.

6. Benedict Joseph Flaget (1763–1850), a French-born Sulpician priest, came to America in 1792 and soon after was sent by Bishop Carroll to the Indian missions. In 1795 he was recalled to Baltimore and then sent to Georgetown College, where he taught French and geography, acting also as the college's vice president. In 1808 he was appointed bishop of the newly created Diocese of Bardstown, Kentucky, a position he tried to refuse. However in 1810 he acquiesced and was consecrated bishop by the then–Archbishop Carroll.

7. Francis Matignon (1753–1818), one of the many prelates who left revolutionary France by way of England, arrived in Baltimore in 1792 and soon after was sent by Bishop Carroll to Boston, where there were no priests and the Catholics were very few, and almost all of them of the working class. He nevertheless labored strenuously,

managing in the end to build the first Catholic Church with the financial help, as well, of many non-Catholics.

8. Jean Louis Lefebvre de Cheverus (1768–1836), was invited by Father Matignon to come to America also by way of England, where he had sought refuge. He joined Matignon in Boston and in 1808 was appointed the first bishop of the Boston Diocese (consecrated in 1810).

9. The Penobscot Indians, presently organized as a Nation, were found mainly in Maine, and together with the Abenaki, Maliseet, Mi'kmaq, and the Passamaquoddy spoke variants of the common Algonquian language and were joined in the Wabanaki Confederacy. During the Revolutionary War, they sided with the American revolutionists against England.

10. John Connolly (1751–1825) was born in Monknewtown, Ireland. He was appointed and consecrated bishop of New York in 1814, serving in this capacity until his death.

11. Matthew Carr (1755–1820), a leading figure in the Order of Saint Augustine in North America, came from Dublin in 1796.

12. Demetrius Augustine Gallitzin (1770–1840), a Russian aristocrat and a priest, was a son of the Russian ambassador to the Netherlands, arriving in the United States in 1792. After attending Saint Mary's Seminary in Baltimore, in 1795 he was ordained a priest. Soon after he was sent to the Allegheny Mountains, where, in 1799, he founded Loretto, now a borough in Cambria County, Pennsylvania.

13. This was designed by the British-born architect Benjamin Henry Latrobe (1764–1820), who also designed the US Capitol in Washington. The Baltimore Basilica, which was erected between 1806 and 1863, has the distinction of being the first Catholic cathedral ever built in the United States.

14. Francis Malevè, (1770–1822) was a native of Louvain, Belgium. Having arrived in the United States in 1809, he was sent to Frederick to replace Father John Dubois, the founder of Mount Saint Mary College and the third Catholic bishop of New York. He expanded the community and was instrumental in establishing a number of parishes and in erecting a Catholic church on a tract of land that had belonged to Charles Carroll of Carrolton's family. Upon his untimely death in 1822, probably due to a cholera epidemic, he was replaced by the Irish Father John McElroy, who remained in Frederick for twenty-three years and later founded Boston College.

15. Louis William Valentine Dubourg (1766–1833) was a Sulpician father who became a bishop in Saint Louis. Born in Haiti of a French family, he was educated in France and ordained a priest in 1790. In 1793, like many French clerics he fled the Revolution and from Spain left for the United States. When he arrived in Baltimore, John Carroll sent him to Georgetown, where he served as president from 1796 to 1799. He then left for Saint Mary College, where he served for thirteen years as that institution's president. In 1812 he was named apostolic administrator of Louisiana and the Floridas. In 1815 he returned to France, then came back in 1817 to be appointed bishop of Saint Louis, and in 1822 was transferred to New Orleans. In 1825 he returned once

more to France, where he was first appointed bishop of Montauban and was later promoted to the archbishopric of Besançon.

16. Saint Mary's Seminary and University, founded in 1791 in Baltimore, and Mount Saint Mary College (now Mount Saint Mary University), founded in 1808 in Emmitsburg.

17. A Dominican, Edward Dominic Fenwick (1768–1832), born in Saint Mary County, Maryland. After returning from Belgium, where he was educated, he was sent to minister in the newly acquired territories west of the Alleghenies, first to Kentucky and later to Ohio. In 1817 he was joined in the ministry by his nephew, Nicholas Dominic Young (1793–1878), also a Dominican priest. In 1822 Father Fenwick was appointed and consecrated first bishop of Cincinnati, and there in 1829 founded the Athenaeum, which later was renamed Saint Francis Xavier Seminary, and was renamed again in 1851 Mount Saint Mary Seminary of the West.

18. Felix de Andreis (1778–1820), a Vincentian priest, in 1816 led a number of Italian Vincentian clerics, Religious Brothers (not ordained priests), and some seminarians to America, traveling first to the Seminary of Saint Thomas in Kentucky and then, in 1817, reaching Saint Louis, where he was appointed vicar general. Later, he and some confreres set off for the newly acquired Louisiana Territory, in 1818 founding Perryville, Missouri, and a seminary named Saint Mary of the Barrens, as such the first institution of higher learning west of the Mississippi. However, due to the fact that the order did not approve the intermingling of seminarians with lay students, the seminary was shut down in 1835.

19. Settled by the English in the seventeenth century, the town laid out on the Port Tobacco River was at one point the second-largest town in Maryland. Its importance declined when the river became less navigable because of excessive silting.

20. Established in 1799, the Georgetown Visitation Convent was the first Catholic school for girls, and the first such institution in the United States. The historical complex is located at 1500 35th Street NW in Washington. The nuns of the Visitation Order are commonly known as Visitation Sisters.

21. John Dubois (1764–1842), a French priest, came to America in 1791, landing in Norfolk, and spent some years in Virginia, until 1794, when he was sent by Bishop John Carroll as pastor to Frederick, in Western Maryland, and to attend as well to the spiritual needs of Catholics living in the Appalachian Mountains region. In 1826, not without some controversy, he was appointed and consecrated as the third bishop of the New York Diocese.

22. Charles Nerinckx (1761–1824) was born in Belgium and was educated at the University of Louvain. In 1804 he came to the United States and was assigned by Bishop Carroll as an assistant to Father Stephen Théodore Badin, the only priest in Kentucky, who has the distinction of being the first ordained priest in the United States. Father Nerinckx was indefatigable in organizing Catholic congregations and in constructing new churches, but he shunned honors, and when the pope sought to promote him to be bishop of New Orleans, he declined.

23. In the book, "Thayer" is misspelled "Their." John Thayer (1755–1815) was born in Boston of a Puritan family. He attended Yale, becoming a Congregationalist minister, and served as a chaplain of a revolutionary military company led by John Hancock. In 1781 he traveled to Europe, and in Italy he was befriended by a Jesuit father who, in 1783, was instrumental in converting him to Catholicism. He then went to Paris to study for the priesthood, and in 1789 he was ordained a priest. In 1790 he returned to the United States. However, in 1803 he went back to Europe, settling in Ireland until his death.

24. Ambrose Maréchal (1768–1828), born in France in 1792, was ordained a Sulpician priest and that same year traveled to the United States. Shortly after his arrival, he was first sent to the Mission of Saint Mary County and then to the Eastern Shore of Maryland. In 1799 he began teaching at Baltimore's Saint Mary's Seminary, and in 1801 he joined Georgetown College's faculty. In 1817 he was appointed coadjutor bishop for Archbishop Neale in Baltimore, whom he succeeded after the latter prelate's death.

25. The title of "Most Christian King" (Roi très Chretien) applied to the kings of France. The king who donated the two paintings to the Baltimore cathedral was Louis XVIII (1755–1824). Joseph Cardinal Fesch (1763–1839), prince of France, was an uncle of Napoleon Bonaparte and like him he, too, was born in Corsica. He was a noted art collector and the founder of the Fesch Musée in Ajaccio.

26. Filed on January 1, 1792. See *The Laws of Maryland from the End of the Year* 1789, compiled by Judge William Kilty (1757–1821) and others.

27. Pre-Civil War legislation forbade legally recognized marriages between slaves, and even if a slave owner consented for two slaves to form a union, such a union was not legally protected. Slaves were considered chattel, and as chattel could not enjoy any legal rights. Often whether a slave master, being he, or it, a Catholic or Protestant individual or an institution, bore little significance on the treatment of slaves. See Darlene C. Goring, "The History of Slave Marriage in the United States," *John Marshall Law Review* (Louisiana State University Law Center) no. 262 (2006): 299–347.

A CONTEMPORARY *UNICUM*:
THE *NORTH AMERICAN REVIEW*
PIECE OF 1823

The important, seldom cited if at all contemporary book review of Father Grassi's *Notizie* appeared, unsigned, in the April 23, 1823, issue of the *North American Review* literary magazine (vol. 39, New Series, no. 14, 229–41). However, the *General Index of the North American Review, Volumes I–CXXV*, 1815–1877—compiled by William Cushing, assistant librarian at the Harvard College Public Library, and published in 1878 by the Cambridge Press of John Wilson and Son—indicates that the review was written by Edward Brooks (1784–1859), an acute but controversial polemicist and pamphleteer, today better remembered for the correspondence jointly published with John A. Lowell (1798–1881), who took it upon himself to have portions of Grassi's work translated into English. The edition of *Notizie* that Brooks reviewed was the 1819 second one that followed the 1818 Roman edition and that was published in Milan. Apparently the third and revised last Turin edition of 1822 had not yet made its way to America; nor do I know if Grassi ever read or was aware of Brooks's review.

NORTH AMERICAN REVIEW
No. XXXIX
NEW SERIES, NO. XW
APRIL 1823

Art. XVI.—*Notizie varie sullo stato presente della Republica degli Stati Uniti dell' America settentrionale, scritte, al principio del 1818, dal Padre Giovanni Grassi, della compagnia di Gesù.* Edizione seconda. Milano, 1819.

A book of travels in the United States, written by a Jesuit, published at Rome, and reprinted at Milan, is in itself a novelty not to be passed over without notice. These are not the only peculiarities of the publication now under consideration. It is recommended by a still more extraordinary circumstance: it is a *pamphlet.* This we mention as matter of congratulation to our readers, not doubting that they will fully participate in the complacency with which, after the scores of folios, quartos, and octavos we have had to grapple withal, we hail the appearance of this literary anomaly, "a pamphlet of travels." They need not to be reminded that amplification is the crying fault of writers of the present day. So rare, indeed, is the opposite quality become, that we are almost ready to pronounce the *"densus et brevis"* in composition, like charity among the virtues, the sum and substance of all excellence. We may, however, solace ourselves with the reflection, that the fault we complain of is not peculiar to our own times; at least we may infer as much from the practice of those sturdy reviewers, the curate and barber in Don Quixote, who have left us an admirable sample of practical criticism. We are informed that these worthies, after having condemned a great number of authors, one by one, to the flames, at length, "without giving themselves the trouble of reading any more titles, ordered the housekeeper to dismiss *all the large books* into the yard." We do not intend to hint that it will ever become expedient to purge our modern libraries after the manner of these primitive critics, but merely to premise, that if we are more indulgent to this "little book," than strict justice would seem to require, we think it a sufficient apology, that it does not offend in the particular above mentioned.

Father Grassi, the author of this treatise, resided some years in
the United States, in the capacity of superior of the Catholic seminary
at Georgetown in the District of Columbia. On his return he was
persuaded by his friends to publish the result of his observations, with
a view, as his editor expresses it, "to give an idea of the rapid progress
that country is already making in commerce, population, manufactures,
the Catholic religion, and every other species of improvement." This
last topic and the subjects connected with it occupy a large portion
of the book; the remainder being principally made up of very general
statements relating to the climate, soil, and productions of the United
States, taken from the common statistical tables, and from a letter of
our obliging countryman, Dr. Mitchell. These are interspersed with
such personal observations as the reverend author had opportunity to
make within the limits of the District of Columbia—for he does not
appear to have extended his researches far beyond them—together with
the gossip of the vulgar, which he has adopted with a degree of credulity
altogether surprising. We have had our doubts, so extravagant are some
of the absurdities detailed by father Grassi, whether he had himself
been duped, or had a mind to make his countrymen a little merry at our
expense. The latter conclusion would have been the most desirable, as
being more honorable to the writer, and by no means offensive to ourselves, for we are so much the friends of good humor, as to be ready to
forgive it under almost any shape. But the profession of the author and
the grave character of the work forbad this interpretation. We leave it
to our readers to determine, from the translations we propose to give of
certain portions of the book, what foundation there is for the first supposition. The coarse jests and broad caricatures, which the good father
has, with overweening simplicity, retailed, are not quoted either for
their novelty or spirit. We have thought it not amiss, however, to take
this opportunity to show how much of the misrepresentation we impute
to foreigners is the reflected picture, which in the excitement of party
animosity or local prejudice, we have drawn of ourselves. While the various sects, religious and political, as well as the different sections of our
country, are but too willing to paint their neighbors in ridiculous, not
to say odious colors, it should not be matter of surprise or complaint,
that their distorted portraits are copied by the credulous or illiberal
traveller, to the infinite disadvantage of our national character. That
the feelings of father Grassi are unfriendly to us, as a nation, we are

far from believing; on the contrary, his observations, on points where his religious prejudices do not operate, denote an artlessness of character quite inconsistent with such a presumption. The following remarks will perhaps excite a smile.

"In respect of food, I can truly say, that after having been in most of the countries of Europe, in my judgment, the mass of the people is no where better provided for than in America, where both flesh and fish are very abundant. The French, who have been there, have justly observed, that in the United States one sees literally fulfilled the wish, which did so much honor to Henry IV of France, who was used to declare, 'that he should not think himself happy until each of his subjects had every Sunday a fowl in the pot.' I cannot say that this country is equally well furnished in the article of drink, which consists of *whiskey* (a sort of brandy) rum, and other distilled spirits, mixed with water. Wine is very dear, and beer exceedingly rare."—p. 10.

This reminds us of the remark we have somewhere seen of a French traveller in Ireland:—"Le vin ordinaire de ce pays-ci," he observes, "est un boisson execrable, que l'on appelle *viski.*"

After some further remarks on the productions and resources of the United States, the author proceeds to state generally the number of inhabitants, and then adds:

"About a seventh part of the actual population are negroes, who are held in slavery, in open contradiction to one of the first articles of the general constitution of this republic, which declares freedom to be a privilege inherent in man, and inalienable. It cannot be denied, however, that there are many powerful reasons against granting liberty to the blacks in a mass. It must not be supposed, that the shores of the American republic are at this day disgraced by the inhuman spectacle of ships discharging cargoes of the miserable victims of human avarice. The present race of negroes in the United States are the descendants of those Africans, who in former times were transported from their native country to the colonies of the New World. The importation of slaves from abroad is now prohibited under severe penalties, but nevertheless, the internal traffic in these unhappy beings still continues. Men are sold to their fellow men, and in the land of liberty, we but too often hear the mournful clank of servile chains. In many states the negroes are kindly treated, and better fed than the peasants of Europe, but in many others they are left in a total ignorance of religion; no attention is paid to their morals; they are never baptized, nor joined in the holy bands of wedlock. The sordid master asks but their labor, and then leaves them like brutes to the blind impulse of their passions, and to follow vices and superstitions that exceed belief. This applies principally to the southern states; in the more northern ones, slavery is abolished, and the example begins by degrees to be imitated elsewhere."—p. 17.

As a counterpart to the foregoing, we shall translate a sketch from the north, which occurs afterwards in describing the character of the people of our country.

"Among the inhabitants of the United States, those of New England are regarded as thorough knaves, practised in the most artful deception, and are nicknamed *Yankis*. The great number of small dealers, who distribute themselves from this quarter into all the other states, and resort to every art and device to get money, has brought this reputation upon the Yankis, an appellation which the English bestow indiscriminately on all Americans. 'It is very certain,' adds the doctor, 'that to deal with this sort of people, requires no little shrewdness and a pretty exact acquaintance with their laws in relation to contracts. But it seems to me,' he adds with an appearance of candor, which we fear he did not learn at Georgetown, 'it seems to me unjust to apply a reproach, which belongs to individuals, or at most to a class of persons, to all the inhabitants of those states.'"—p. 29.

After the preceding samples, the reader will not be entirely unprepared for the following description of American manners.

"The unrestrained freedom which obtains, the drunkenness which abounds, the rabble of adventurers, the great number of negro slaves, the almost infinite variety of sects, and the little real religion that is met with, the incredible number of novels that are read, and the insatiate eagerness for gain, are indeed circumstances, that would hardly give reason to expect much in point of manners. At first view, however, one is not aware of the depravity of this country, because it is hidden for a time under the veil of an engaging exterior. But it is not difficult to discern it, when a little familiar with the inhabitants, particularly in the cities. The vices of gaming and drunkenness prevail there to a degree altogether incredible in Italy, and frequently prove fatal in their consequences, not only to the individual, but to whole families. Their general intercourse is civil, but notwithstanding this civility, not a few among them commit frequent breaches of good manners. To pare the nails, for instance, or comb the head in company; to sit with the feet resting, on the nearest chair, or braced against the wall in the air, are not considered indecorous. When a stranger is introduced into company, he is pointed out by name, and presented in turn to each individual present. Friends who meet, even after an absence of many years, never embrace, but merely shake hands. Mothers have the laudable habit of nursing their own children, a custom which would be still more praiseworthy, if performed with a little more reserve. The richest individuals do not disdain to hold the plough or the spade in their own fields, and to take their meals with the laborers. Luxury in dress is carried to a degree hardly known in Europe; they dress in the country with the same expense as in town, and on holidays rich clothing forms not the smallest indication of the circumstances of the wearer.

"Dancing is the most common recreation in America, where the passion for this diversion seems to be even as strong as in France. An absurd point of honor gives rise to frequent duels, and to evade the rigor of the laws, the parties retire to the frontiers of some neighbouring state for the purpose of deciding their quarrels in this barbarous, shocking, and superstitious manner, in which the aggressor is frequently triumphant, and the injured party has the satisfaction to be left wounded, crippled, or perchance dead."—p. 30

We take from the author's remarks on education those which relate to the female sex.

"The education of young ladies rarely consists in learning the use of the needle or the spindle, or in working linen or woollen stuffs; but as soon as they are taken from the English school, they never fail to learn to dance, and sometimes a few lessons in music, drawing, and perhaps French complete their education. It is of no moment that this is forgotten in the course of a few weeks. Their vanity is satisfied in being able to say that they have studied music, drawing, and French."—p. 25.

From the observations on literature we select those which relate to public speaking, as the most remarkable.

"Greek and Latin are generally cultivated, but with very few exceptions, not in a sufficient degree to give a perception or taste for the beauties of the great masters of Greece and Italy, otherwise could it be possible that in the public prints they should boast of the Columbiad of Barlow, as a poem equal, nay superior, to Homer and Virgil, and the speeches of their representatives as models of eloquence infinitely

above those of Demosthenes and Cicero?* It is not to be denied, that
the Americans express themselves with great facility and elegance, and
sometimes display fine traits of real eloquence. In short, after gold, this
is their idol; but of the various branches, which, according to the greatest masters, make up the art of speaking well, elocution is the one on
which they bestow the greatest care. Provided a speaker or writer deals
in choice expressions, elegant phrases, and harmonious periods, nothing more is required to stamp him as a great orator, however deficient
he may be in the richness of invention, felicity of thought, weight of
sentiment, force of argument, accuracy of arrangement, and command
of the passions, which would be required elsewhere."—p. 39

In the foregoing extracts, the reader has found little to flatter national vanity; but we have translated them, not only with a view to show
how much injustice may be done with the most honest intentions, but
because we think his discrimination will discern, through a great deal of
prejudice and misapprehension, not a little wholesome truth. It cannot
be necessary to comment upon this part of father Grassi's treatise. If
we feel that any of his strictures are just, we have only to profit by them,
and where we know them to be otherwise, it can give little satisfaction
to ourselves, and will add nothing to our real merit, to refute them.
We now proceed to notice the reverend author's observations on the
religious character of the United States; and here we are sorry to be
obliged to say, that on this subject, although he loses none of his credulity, be leaves all his candor and moderation behind him. It must not
be supposed that, at this period of the world, we look for a great degree
of either of the above qualities in theological discussions. But we own
we did not expect to see stale jokes from the jest books brought out and
gravely applied in illustration of the religious character of a nation. We
admit that, if one half the abuse which father Grassi complains of has
been bestowed upon the Catholics by the American protestants, the
account stands pretty fairly balanced between them. This, however,
is not to our present purpose, and we do not intend to enter into the
controversy any further than to explain the feelings which dictated the

---

* It were well if this rodomontade were confined to newspapers, but strangers
may well call our taste in question when they see a grave biographer quote,
as a most happy illustration of the powers of a late distinguished southern
orator, what was said of him by another orator from the same state, namely,
that "he was Shakspeare and Garrick combined."

following statements. After bestowing due praise on the perfect toleration, which is not only professed but observed in the United States, he
proceeds to remark:

"Among the peculiarities of America which have attracted the
notice of travellers, few are more striking than, that people frequently
live for years together without ever knowing the religion of each other,
and when interrogated upon that point they do not answer, I *believe*,
but I was *brought up* in such a sect or religion. But in order to give a
better idea of the consideration in which religion is held, I shall state
a few facts. There was a regiment stationed at Georgetown, a suburb
of the flourishing city of Washington, and among other regulations
the soldiers were required to attend church every sabbath. But as they
were of various persuasions, it was difficult to determine what church
or congregation they should attend. So the affair was compromised
in the following way. They went the first Sunday to the Catholic
Chapel, the next to the Methodists, on the third to the English, then
to the Calvinists, and so on through them all in succession. It is not
uncommon to find persons who have professed all the *sects*, and the
reasons for these changes are diverting enough. A young lady related of
herself, that she took it into her head that that must needs be the best
religion whose professors were the most genteel folks in the city. She
was brought up in I know not what sect, but observing every Sunday a
greater number of carriages before the congregational meeting-house
than any where else, she forthwith became a Congregationalist. Her
parents changed their place of residence, and she her religion, because
she observed more carriages near the English Church. The family
again removed, and by the standard of carriages she was again converted. At length she was married, and took the creed of her husband.
It is not uncommon to see parents who do not think it best to instruct
their children in the principles of Christianity, but are satisfied with
giving them notions of natural honesty, observing, that the children
at the proper time can choose the sect that shall be most to their taste;
accordingly, you may frequently see in a family as many sects as individuals. In New England the sects are more rigid than elsewhere,
consequently various superstitions and vain observances are there most
in vogue, and the *Sticks Doctors*, or 'doctors of the rods,' find here the
greatest encouragement for their impositions."—p. 63.

What particular class of dignitaries is intended by father Grassi

under the English name of *Sticks Doctors*, or *"dottori dalle bacchette,"*
we are entirely unable to conjecture, although we have run over all the
titles of honor in law, physic, and divinity, in which, thanks to the liberality of our literary institutions, we may hold up our heads with any
nation, ancient or modern. Perhaps some of our readers may be able to
furnish an explanation for themselves.

"Notwithstanding," continues our author, "the indifference which
prevails among these various sects, there appears, particularly at the
north, a great display of piety. Every body reads the bible, and in New-
England no traveller, not excepting a courier, is allowed to proceed on
his journey on Sunday, and they are every year presenting memorials
to Congress to prohibit travelling on the Lord's day. The captain of
the vessel in which I sailed from America to Europe, would not allow
the passengers to play at *Domino*, nor sing on the Sabbath, at the same
time that he permitted all sorts of indecency and profanity among the
sailors, and happening to arrive in port on a Sunday morning, he kept
them hard at work all day without the smallest necessity. Anciently
the observance of fasts at the north was carried to a most extravagant
height. There still remain in several states laws relating to religious
worship, which insist strongly on the observance of the third commandment. These laws, though still in existence, are not now strictly
enforced, and are called Blue Laws, of which the following may serve as
a specimen. 'To the end that the Sabbath may be more exactly observed,
it is enjoined on those who intend to go to church, to saddle their horses
the day before. On fast days the ladies will not be permitted to scour
the floor, make the beds, or comb the children's heads—No beer to be
made on the Saturday, lest it should work on the Sunday.'"—p. 68.

We regret that the wag who furnished the doctor with these extracts should have given him so poor a sample of this venerable code,
for we think there is scarce a lad of any cleverness among us who would
not have been able to invent a better. Having displayed a general view
of the state of religion among us, father Grassi attempts to enumerate the different sects in the United States, which he names in Italian
as follows: Congregazionalisti, Metodisti, Anglicani, Presbiteriani,
Anabaptisti, Univcrsalisti, Unitari, Luterani, Puritani, Quacqueri,
Dunkers e Chrystiani. All these are passed upon in turn, with appropriate denunciations, and the author then proceeds to consider the style
of preaching in our country.

"The passion for elegant preaching is universal in this nation, and some traveller has remarked, that religion here reduces itself into the mere fondness for fluent preachers. Hence the great end of their ministers is preaching, that is to say, a polished diction, which flatters and sooths the ear; their sermons are more commonly the essays of philosophers, than the discourses of Christian pastors, and not unfrequently political rhapsodies, suited to the taste of the majority of the audience. They affect an air of great indifference, to which they give the plausible name of liberality towards other sects, but commonly conclude with 'my hearers, stick to your own.' That the Catholic religion is the only one which rarely participates in their liberality, will not appear strange to those who are acquainted with them. It is indeed matter of surprise, that men of honest principles, and some of them not without sense and information, should persist in the grossest prejudices and the most absurd errors in regard to the Catholic religion. Our astonishment will subside, however, when we reflect, that in addition to the force of education, and early impressions, the circumstances of the American protestants are very different from those of the German and English. In these countries the walls of their temples, the inscriptions on the tombs of their ancestors, the sacred relics that are preserved, the many monuments which still exist, the books that are in his hands remind the protestant that he has renounced the religion of his fathers, and reproach him as it were with his heresy and apostasy. But in America, there is nothing of all this—all is new, and in many parts they have heard nothing for two hundred years but a repetition of the prejudices and calumnies against the Catholics, which their fathers have handed down to them; there, a catechism is never seen; there, so much as a Catholic preacher is never heard."

Had our author confined himself to remarks like the foregoing, we should not have thought him deserving of very serious reprehension. That a stranger, particularly a native of a Catholic country, should be surprised, not to say scandalized, at the little regard that is here paid to the established modes of belief, and the apparent indifference that prevails as to forms of worship, is not wonderful. We admit the fact, and are by no means prepared to repel the censure. It is one of the evils incident to unlimited toleration. We should be glad to find as good an apology for the insertion of low and vulgar abuse, which is applied to particular sects merely on the authority of some prating story-teller, or scandalous newspaper. We select an instance from his account of the Methodists.

"I have seen in print the following dialogue between a shopkeeper and his domestic, both Methodists. *William*, have you sanded the sugar, lad? Yes, sir. Have you watered the spirit? Yes, sir. Have you wet the tobacco well? Yes, sir.—Come to prayers, then."

We shall take two other anecdotes of the same character, which we think will suffice.

"Three years ago a minister of the Church of England in Maryland, substituted cider (a liquor made of apple juice) for wine in the ceremony of the Lord's Supper. The fraud being afterwards detected, and charged upon him, he replied with the utmost coolness, 'that wine was dear, and it was all the same thing.' One of their ministers confessed candidly, that the Catholic religion was the true one, but he had four strong objections to it. Pray what are they? he was asked. A wife and three children to support, was his reply."

We believe our readers are by this time pretty well apprized of what father Grassi considers canonical. His doctrine of reform is simple, if it has no other recommendation. If his word may be taken, our course is plain before us, and but one thing is wanting to draw us from the depths of barbarism and heresy to the safe ground of orthodoxy and refinement. We cannot but respect the zeal of father Grassi, and have no doubt he is perfectly sincere in his professions. We are really afraid, however, that Martin and Jack are not yet prepared to take it for truth, even upon the assurance of Peter, "that bread contains the quintessence of beef, mutton, veal, venison, partridge, plum pudding, and custard." The work closes with an account of the various Catholic establishments, and a general view of the progress and present state of that religion in this country. The following description of their principal seminaries. and religious houses is not without interest.

"The fathers of the society of Jesus, besides their missions, have in Georgetown, near Washington, in a charming situation, a College for the education of youth, which was authorised by an act of the first of March, 1815, to confer academical degrees, as is done by other colleges and universities in this country. It is owing to a want of students that this order has not kept up the school they opened at New York, under the title of the Literary Institution, where they still own the building destined to that use. The priests of St Sulpice have a respectable college

at Baltimore, on which the Legislature of Maryland has bestowed
the privileges of an university. They have also a house of education at
Emitzburg. The English Dominicans have a convent in Kentucky,
with a school and church under the title of St Rosa di Lima, and in
1816 had four students in theology, besides a few probationers. Several
gentlemen have lately arrived from Italy in the western states, from
the mission of St Vincenzo di Paolo, and are only waiting the arrival of
the bishop of New Orleans to commence an establishment. There are,
besides these, several other religious communities in America, the most
ancient of which is the nunnery of mendicant Carmelites, of the reform
of St Teresa. Three nuns of this order had the courage to leave their
English convent at Antwerp, and cross the great Atlantic to establish
a nunnery here; in a few years their numbers increased to twenty-six.
Their nunnery, which is entirely of wood, is situated near Port Tobacco
in Maryland. Archbishop Neal, full of zeal for the education of youth,
has established in Georgetown a society of nuns of visitation, who
superintend the religious education of little girls. In a short time this
society increased to the degree, that last summer it consisted of thirty-
six nuns. Another establishment for the same object has been founded
by the Abbe Dubois in Emitzburg. Some of these sisters have gone
from Emitzburg to Philadelphia, where they have the care of a found-
ling hospital, whose little inmates they lead on holy festivals in good
order some times to one church, and sometimes to another, to the great
delight and edification of the public, and with some advantage to the
charity, 'which is supported by the alms of Catholics and several benevolent protestants. The truly zealous abbé Nerinx: has founded a nunnery in Kentucky, which is called the 'Sisterhood of Mary at the foot
of the Cross.' Lastly, the abbé Their [Thayer?] who from a Calvinistic
preacher became a Catholic at Rome, and died lately in Ireland, has left
a fund sufficient to establish in Boston, his native place, a convent of
Ursulines for the education of young women."

   This relation will give some idea of the exertions the Catholics have
been and are still making to diffuse their doctrines in this country. The
return of his holiness to Rome, after his unhappy and atrocious exile,
seemed a fit occasion to be signalized by a reform in the church, and an
attempt to restore its tottering authority. One of the first steps towards
the attainment of this object was the revival of the order of Jesuits,
which had by its zeal, perseverance, and admirable discipline added

greatly to the influence and grandeur of the church. The persecuted remnant of this once powerful order, which had survived their day of adversity, repaired to the holy see, and soon evinced by their ardor and industry, that they had not lost their distinguishing characteristics. The other orders and religious communities, which had been dispersed by the French, were reassembled, and the affairs of the church assumed a tone of spirit and animation to which they had been long unaccustomed. Nor was this excitement confined to the restoration of the establishment in Italy, or even in Europe. The effects of it have extended themselves to our own country, where the missionaries from Rome have been active and vigilant. Their efforts, as we have already seen, and the experience of every day convinces us, have not been without success. How far they may continue to be successful, we are unable to foresee, nor do we think it of much moment to inquire. Although we do not expect from their labors the golden harvest which father Grassi seems to promise himself, we are still far from regarding them with the apprehension and anxiety, which some of our fellow citizens appear to entertain. The assertion of father Grassi is certainly in a degree true, that there has heretofore existed in this country an unwarrantable prejudice against Catholics, which (we say it with shame) is not yet eradicated. That a dread of papacy should at one period have been entertained is not surprising, but it is surely time to have done with it. The temporal supremacy of the pope, and the other bug-bears, which are regularly marshalled to fright the good protestants of England from consenting to Catholic emancipation, have no terrors for us. Are we reminded of the extravagance and impolicy of their institutions? In answer, we will merely ask, have they not all been outdone by the fanciful vagaries, the incredible inventions of modern protestants? It will hardly become any persuasion to object to the tenets of another, until we can say with certainty where the exuberant ingenuity of man will stop. For ourselves, we welcome Catholicism, or any other sect, so long as it shall he recommended, to use the words of our author, "by that mild and persuasive charity, which marks the true ministers of Jesus Christ." Good policy, as well as brotherhood, requires that the numerous emigrants who flock to us should be encouraged, rather than otherwise, in their national belief. We need not look beyond our own city for the good effects of a Catholic establishment, under the guidance of mild, enlightened, and exemplary pastors. We are not to ask ourselves whether we should prefer to make new comers Presbyterians, Lutherans, or Quakers, according to our belief, but whether we will have them Christians or not. The foreigner, who comes among us, and finds the faith in which he was educated unknown or despised, who looks around in vain for the worship he has been taught to revere—is it to be supposed that he will readily adopt any of the sects he finds about him, all of them perhaps equally revolting to his conscience? Every one finds an answer in his own breast. He will probably become indifferent to religion, and insensible to its sanctions; he may become an infidel—he will rarely become a convert. As friends of toleration, we never look with jealousy on the growth of a weak sect. The multiplication of creeds, which, according to our author, is viewed by many with alarm, as the germ of future discord, is regarded by us in a very different point of view. Despairing of unanimity in matters of faith, we look for the preservation of religious quiet in the infinite variety of belief. The maxim of the poet, that

All nature's difference makes all nature's peace

may with strict analogy be applied to the present case. With these sentiments we consider every new sect as adding strength to the common barrier against religious tyranny. Weakness is always tolerant; but we shall think the death blow of religious freedom given, the moment that anyone sect, be it which it may, is strong enough to dictate to the rest.

BIBLIOGRAPHY

Barringer, G. M. "They Came to Georgetown: The Italians." *Georgetown Today*, March 1977, 17–19.

Becket, J. A. "Georgetown University." *The Cosmopolitan* 9 (1890): 449–59.

Botta, Carlo. *Storia della Guerra dell'Indipendenza degli Stati Uniti di America* (History of the War of Independence of the United States of America). Paris, 1809.

Curran, R. E. *The Bicentennial History of Georgetown University.* Vol. 1, *From Academy to University,* 1789–1889. Washington, DC: Georgetown University Press, 1993.

———. "Splendid Poverty: Jesuit Slaveholding in Maryland, 1805–1838." In *Catholics in the Old South: Essays on Church and Culture,* edited by Randall M. Miller and Jon L. Wakelyn, 125–46. Macon, GA: Mercer University Press, 1983.

Daley, J. M. *Georgetown University: Origin and Early Years.* Washington, DC: Georgetown University Press, 1957.

De Pauw, Cornelius. *Recherches philosophiques sur les Americains: Ou mémoires intéressants pour servir à l'histoire de l'espèce humaine* (Philosophical Studies on the Americans: Or an Interesting Account to Be Used toward a Compilation of a History of Human Kind). Berlin, n.d.; London, 1768.

Devitt, E. I. "Georgetown in the Early Days." *Records of the Columbia Historical Society* 12 (1909): 21–37.

Dickens, Charles. *American Notes.* London: Chapman & Hall, 1842.

Durkin, J. T. *Georgetown University: First in the Nation's Capital.* Garden City, NY: Doubleday, 1964.

Garraghan, G. J. "John Anthony Grassi, SJ, 1775–1849." *Catholic Historical Review* 21, no. 11 (1937): 273–92.

Grassi, G. A. *Diary* (photostat copy) and *Miscellanea Papers.* Georgetown University Archives, Catholic Historical MSS Collection, box 3, folders 11 and 12, no date.

———. "Journal d'un voyage vers la Chine" (written c. 1836). Unsigned translation, "Voyage of the Very Rev. Fr. John Grassi, SJ, from Russia to America. Jan. 1805–Oct. 1810." *Woodstock Letters* 4 no. 1 (1875): 115–36.

———. *Notizie sullo stato presente della Repubblica degli Stati Uniti dell'America settentrionale*, 3rd and final rev. ed. Turin: Chirio & Mina, 1822.

Guilday, P. K. *The Life and Times of John Carroll, Archbishop of Baltimore (1735–1815)*, 2 vols. New York: Encyclopedia Press, 1922.

Hanley, John, ed. *The John Carroll Papers*, vol. 3 (Notre Dame, IN: University of Notre Dame Press, 1976).

Horace. *Satires, Epistles, and Ars Poetica*, trans. H. R. Fairclough. Loeb Classical Library 194. Cambridge, MA: Harvard University Press, 1966.

March, José M., SJ. *El Restaurador de la Compañia de Jesus, Beato José Pignatelli y su tiempo*, vols. 1 and 2. Barcelona: Imprenta Rivista Iberica, 1935, 1944.

Mazzei, Filippo. *Recherches historiques et politiques sur les États-Unis de l'Amerique Septentrionale* (Historical and Political Studies on the United States in Northern America). 4 vols. 1788.

McElroy, J. "An Account of the Re-establishment of the Society in the United States and of Events Connected Therewith, Written in 1863–64." *Woodstock Letters* 16, no. 1 (1887): 161–68.

McGucken, W. *The Jesuits and Education*. Milwaukee: Bruce, 1932.

Pellico, Silvio. *Le mie prigioni* (My Prisons, or My Imprisonment). 1832.

Pizzorusso, G. "Giovanni Antonio Grassi." In *Dizionario Biografico degli Italiani*, vol. 58. Rome: Treccani, 2002.

Ryan, J. J. "Reminiscences of Some Distinguished Men of Science Connected in the Past with Georgetown College." *Woodstock Letters* 30, no. 1 (1901): 94–103.

Tropea, Joseph L., James Edward Miller, and Cheryl Beattie-Repetti, eds. *Support and Struggle: Italians and American-Italians in Comparative Perspective* (Staten Island, NY: The Association, 1986).

Unsigned papers. "Bishop Plaget Applies for Two of Ours to Be Bishops, Some Unpublished Letters." *Woodstock Letters* 28, no. 1 (1899): 72–77.

———. "Papers Relating to the Early History of the Maryland Mission." *Woodstock Letters* 4, 1875.

———. "The Suppression and Restoration of the Society." *Woodstock Letters* 10, no. 2 (1881): 89–91.

TAVOLA

Delle cose più rimarcabili nella Geografia degli Stati-Uniti dell'America Settentrionale.

	STATI O TERRITORJ	SITUAZIONE Lat. N.	SITUAZIONE Long.	AREA DI MIGLIA quadrati.	PRODOTTI.	MINERALI.	POPOLAZIONE secondo il censo dell'anno 1810.	ABITANTI miglia quadrati.	CAPITALI o città principali.	ABITANTI delle città.	UNIVERSITÀ o COLLEGI.	DEPUTATI al congresso.
1	Maine Massachussets	43 5 41 23	10 00 E 6 55 E	31,750 78,300	Granturco, segala, arena, canapa, lino, e frumento.	Piombo, retriuolo, marmo, e coppa-rosa.	218,705 472,040	9. 69	Portland. Boston.	7,16c 33,25c	Bowdone U. Cambrige U.	20
2	Newhampshire	42 42	6 10 E	11,200.	Grani, frutta, pascoli.	Ferro, zolfo, piom-bo, e rame.	214,460	23	Concord. C. Portsmouth.	2,39: 6,93:	Dartmouth.	6
3	Vermont	42 44	5 27 E	8,700	Grani, frutta, pascoli.	Ferro, piombo, cop-parosa, marmo, e vetriuolo.	217,895	21	Mompellier C. Danville.		Midlebury. Burlington.	6
4	Rhode-Island	41 22	5 5o E	1,500	Come nel Massa-chussets.	Ferro, carbon fos-sile, qualche rame, e calamita.	76,931	37	Providence.	77: 10,071	Brown. V.	2
5	Connecticut	41 00	5 00 E	4,000	Frumento, segala, granturco,orzo,ave-na, lino, canapa.	Ferro, piombo, ra-me, zinco, e un po' di carbon fossile.	261,942	53	Hartford. New-Haven.	3,995 5,772	Yales.	6
6	New-York	40 33	2 43 O	46,000	Frumento, granturc-o, come sopra.	Ferro, piombo, rame zinco,marmo,zolfo, carb. foss., e po' arg.	959,049	15	Albany C. New-York.	9,35c 130,00c	Columbia Schenectfady, ed altre.	27
7	New-Jersey	38 36	5 5 E	6,900	Frumento, segala, etc., e frutta.	Ferro, piombo, ra-me, gesso, carbon foss., ardesia.	245,562	3o	Trenton C. Newark.	3,802 8,008	Princeton ed alt.	7
8	Pensilvania	39 43	3 3o O	42,500	Grani, legumi, e molti frutti, pasco-li.	Ferr.,carb. foss., pie-tre calcare, un poco di piombo, e rame.	810,091	17	Harrisburg C. Philadelphia.	2,287 98,866	University of Pensylvania ed alt.	22
9	Delaware	38 29	1 58 E	1,700	Frumento, pascoli, e frutta.	Ferro.	72,674	35	Dover C. Wilmington.	800 4,106		2
10	Maryland	38 00	2 3o O	10,800	Frumento, grano, tabacco, frutta, e poco cotone.	Ferro, e qualche carbon fossile.	380,546	27	Annapolis C. Baltimore.	2,000 56,356	Abington S.t Mary's Annapolis.	9
11	Virginia	36 3o	6 26 O	61,000	Frumento, tabac-co, grani, indigo, e un poco di seta.	Ferro, carb. fossile, qualche rame, piom-bago, e oro.	974,622	13	Richmond	9,735	William et Mary	23
12	Ohio	38 3o	7 40 O	39,000	Frumento, grani, e frutta, lino, cana-pa, e cotone.	Ferro, carb. fossile, la pietra calcarea vi abbonda.	230,760	6	Columbus C. Cincinnati.	448 2,540	University of Athens, ed alt.	6
13	Kentucky	36 3o	12 20 O	39,000	Come sopra, e ta-bacco.	Ferro, carb. fossile, piombo, copparosa, alume, e sale.	406,511	10	Frankfort C. Lexington.	1,099 4,326	S. Thmas' Coll.	10
14	Tbenassee	35 00	13 5 O	40,000	Cotone, fromento, fieni, e frutta.	Come sopra, e ni-tro, piombo, e poco argento.	261,727	7	Nashville			6
15	Nord Carolina	33 43	6 5o O	45,000	Cotone, tabacco, grani, frutta, e pa-scoli.	Ferro, cobalto, oro.	555,500	15	Raleigh C. Newhern.	1,000 1,467		13
16	Sud Carolina	32 6	6 25 O	28,700	Cotone, riso, gra-ni, pascoli.	Ferro, ardesia, mar-la, piombo, e rame.	415,115	17	Columbia C. Georgetown.	1,500 2,000	Charlestown ed alt.	9
17	Georgia	3o 3o	9 5 O	58,000	Cotone, frumento, grani, riso, tabacco, e zucchero.	Ocra gialla, e rame	252,433	5	Milledgeville Savannah	1,237 5,215	University of Georgia.	6
18	Luigiana	29 00	17 00 O	48,000	Cotone, zucchero, indigo, e frutta.		76,556	2	New-Orleans.	17,242		1
19	Indiana	37 45	10 47 O	34,000	Grani, pascoli, frut-ta, e cotone nel Sud.	Carbon fossile, sale, e argento.	68,780	1	Corydon C. Vincennes.	670		1
	Distretto di Colombia	39 53	0	100	Frumento, e gran-turco, e frutta.	Ferro.	24,025	240	Washington.	13,000	Georgetown Coll.	0
	Mississipi	3o 15	14 3a O	39,000	Cotone, grani, ri-so, poco zucchero, ed indigo.		65,979	1 ogni 2m	Washington.	1,511		0
20	Illionesi	37 00	14 15 O	50,000	Grani, frutta, pascoli.	Carb. fossile, rame, piombo, e ferro.	12,282	1 ogni 4m	Kaskaskia.	622		1
	Territorio Michigan	41 45	8 18 O	27,000	Frumenti, grani, patate, frutta.		4,762	1 ogni 7m	Detoit.	700		0
	Nord-owest Territorio	41 45	18 5o O	147,000								0
	Territorio del Missouri	36 00	49 3o O	1,580,000	Grani, pascoli, frut-ta, cotone, e poco zucchero, e indigo.		20,845	1 og.100m	S. Louis.	1,600		0
22	Alabama	35 00	8 0 O	46,000	Cotone, riso, ed orzo in abbondanza		29,683		Fort-Stoddart Huntsville.			1
	TOTALI						7,335,575					184

Nota. La longitudine si conta dal meridiano di Washington. Questa città è a 38.d 53.i latit. bor. , e a 76° 55' 24.t di longitudine ovest di Grenwich.

Table of All the Most Remarkable Things to Be Found within the Geography of the United States in North America

	States or Territories	Situation Lat. N.	Long.	Area in sq miles	Produces	Minerals	Population according to the 1810 census	Inhabitants by square miles	Capitals of principal cities	Inhabitants by cities	Universities or colleges	Congressmen
1	Maine	45 5	10 00 E	31,750	Corn, rye, oats, hemp, flax & wheat	Lead, vitriol, marble & copper sulfate	228,705	9	Portland	7,169	Bowdoin College	20
	Massachusetts	41 23	6 55 E	78,300	wheat	copper sulfate	472,040	69	Boston	33,250	Cambridge U.	
2	New Hampshire	42 42	6 10 E	11,200	Cereals, fruit & pastures	Iron, sulfur, lead & copper	214,460	23	Concord C. Portsmouth	2,393 6,934	Dartmouth	6
3	Vermont	42 44	5 27 E	8,700	Cereals, fruit & pastures	Iron, lead, copper sulfate, marble & vitriol	217,895	21	Montpelier C. Danville		Middlebury Burlington	6
4	Rhode Island	42 22	5 50 E	1,500	Same as Massachusetts	Iron, pit coal, some copper & lodestone	76,931	57	Providence	771 10,071	Brown U.	2
5	Connecticut	41 00	5 00 E	4,000	Wheat, rye, corn, barley, oats, flax & hemp	Iron, lead, copper, zinc, marble & some pit coal	261,942	53	Hartford C. New Haven	3,595 5,772	Yale	6
6	New York	42 33	2 45 W	46,000	Wheat, corn as above	Iron, lead, copper, zinc, marble, sulfur, pit coal & some silver	959,049	15	Albany C. New York	9,356 130,000	Columbia Schenectady & others	27
7	New Jersey	38 36	3 5 E	6,900	Wheat, rye, etc. & fruit	Iron, lead, copper, gypsum, pit coal & slate	245,562	30	Trenton C. Newark	3,002 8,008	Princeton & others	7
8	Pennsylvania	39 43	3 30 W	42,500	Cereals, legumes, much fruit & pastures	Iron, pit coal, limestone, some lead & copper	810,091	17	Harrisburg C. Philadelphia	2,287 98,866	University of Pennsylvania & others	22
9	Delaware	38 29	1 58 E	1,700	Wheat, pastures & fruit	Iron	72,674	35	Dover C. Wilmington	800 4,406		2
10	Maryland	38 00	2 30 W	10,800	Wheat, grains, tobacco, fruit, & some cotton	Iron & some pit coal	380,546	27	Annapolis C. Baltimore	2,000 56,556	Abington St. Mary's Annapolis	9
11	Virginia	36 30	6 26 W	64,000	Wheat, tobacco, cereals, indigo & some silk	Iron, pit coal, some copper, graphite & some gold	974,622	13	Richmond	9,735	William and Mary	23
12	Ohio	38 30	7 40 W	39,000	Wheat, cereals, fruit, flax, hemp & cotton	Iron, pit coal, & abundant limestone	230,760	6	Columbus C. Cincinnati	448 2,540	University of Athens & others	6

13	Kentucky	36 30	12 20 W	39,000	As above & tobacco	Iron, pit coal, lead, copper sulfate, alum & salt	406,511	10	Frankfort C. Lexington	1,099 4,326	St. Thomas College	10
14	Tennessee	35 00	13 5 W	40,000	Cotton, wheat, hay & fruit	As above & nitrate, lead & some silver	261,727	7	Nashville			6
15	North Carolina	33 43	6 50 W	45,000	Cotton, tobacco, cereals, fruit & pastures	Iron, cobalt, gold	555,500	15	Raleigh C. Newbern	1,000 1,467		13
16	South Carolina	32 6	6 25 W	28,700	Cotton, rice, cereals & pastures	Iron, slate, marla, lead & copper	415,115	17	Columbia C. Georgetown	1,500 2,000	Charlestown & others	9
17	Georgia	30 30	9 5 W	98,000	Cotton, wheat, cereals, rice, tobacco & sugar	Yellow ochre & copper	252,433	5	Milledgeville Savannah	1,237 5,215	University of Georgia	6
18	Louisiana	29 00	17 00 W	48,000	Cotton, sugar, indigo & fruit		76,556	2	New Orleans	17,242		1
19	Indiana	37 45	10 47 W	34,000	Cereals, pastures, fruit & cotton in the southern part	Pit coal, salt & silver	68,780	1	Corydon C. Vincennes	670		1
	District of Columbia	39 53	0	100	Wheat, corn & fruit	Iron	24,023	240	Washington	13,000	Georgetown College	0
20	Mississippi	30 15	14 32 W	39,000	Cotton, cereals, rice, a little sugar & indigo		65,979	1 every 2 sq. miles	Washington	1,511		0
21	Illinois	37 00	14 15 W	50,000	Cereals, fruit & pastures	Pit coal, copper, lead & iron	12,282	1 every 4 sq miles	Kaskaskia	622		1
	Michigan Territory	41 45	8 18 W	27,000	Wheat, cereals, potatoes & fruit		4,762	1 every 7 sq miles	Detroit	700		0
	North-West Territory	41 45	18 50 W	147,000								0
	Missouri Territory	30 00	49 30 W	1,580,000	Cereals, pastures, fruit, cotton, and a little sugar & indigo		20,845	1 every 100 sq miles	Saint Louis	1,600		0
22	Alabama	35 00	8 W	45,000	Abundant cotton, rice, and barley		29,683		Fort Stoddart Huntsville			1
	Total						7,335,575					184

Please note that the longitude has been calculated from Washington's meridian. This city is located at 38ᵗʰ 53' lat. bor., and at 76°55' 24" longitude west of Greenwich

INDEX

Entries to the table at the end of the book are indicated by "t" following the page numbers.

abolition of slavery, 56n14
Ad majorem Dei gloriam (AMDG), 30, 32n25, 55
Adrain, Robert, 23, 32n21
agriculture and food, xiii, 83, 98–99*t*; agricultural products, 4–5, 29; export commerce of agricultural products, 6; grapes, 4, 30n2; livestock, 29; primary sector in 1790, 30n5; soil and land, 3; technological advances, use of, 4–5
Alabama, 99*t*
Albany, New York, 62
alcoholic beverages. *See* wine and alcoholic beverages
Alexandria, Virginia: Catholics in, 64; as port for commerce, 13
Algonquian language, 76n9
AMDG (*Ad majorem Dei gloriam*), 30, 32n25, 55
America and Americans, use of terms, 2
American Indians, xxixn16, 10–11; fair treatment of, 56n14; Illinois tribes, 63; missionaries needed to work with, 73; Penobscot Indians, 62, 76n9; Wabanaki Confederacy, 76n9
American Ornithology (Wilson), 21, 31n19
American Philosophical Society: *Transactions*, 23
American Revolution, xxxn16, 8, 43, 56n15, 76n9

Anabaptists, 45, 54, 88
Andrei, Giovanni, xix, xx, xxviiin7
Anglicans, 35, 43–44, 88, 90; Congregationalists and, 39–40, 50; deacon leaving and resuming post, 51–52; excommunication by, 49; Methodists keeping some articles of, 40; number of churches in New York City, 54; rejection of Presbyterian ordinations by, 44; Thirty-Nine Articles, 34, 43; Walmesley on, 75n4
anti-Catholicism, xiii, 22, 34, 37–38, 44, 49–50, 73, 89, 92
apostasy, 70–71
apprenticeships, 18, 31n14
Archimedes, 24
architecture, xiii, 14
Ashton, John, xxiv
Associated Reformed Presbyterian Church, 44
astronomy and science, xi, xii, xvii, xviii, 23
Athanasius (saint), 43
Atlantic colonies, settlement of, 8
Augusta, Georgia, Catholics in, 64
avidity. *See* wealth, pursuit of

Badin, Stephen Théodore, 77n22
Baltimore: cathedral (Basilica) in, 64, 67–68, 76n13; Catholic archbishopric in, 61; Catholic orphanage in, 66–67;

Baltimore (*continued*)
    commerce, 5, 13; diocese of, 64; funeral
    of John Carroll in, 60; Grassi's arrival in,
    xviii; Unitarians in, 45
Baltimore, Lord, 10, 60
banking industry, xiii, 6, 7, 15
Bardstown, Kentucky, Catholics in, 60, 61,
    63, 75n6
Barlow, Joel: *Columbiad*, 21–22, 31n17, 85
Beaumont, Gustave de: *Marie: Ou
    l'esclavage aux États-Unis*, xxvi
Berkeley, George, 50, 57n20
Bible, 34, 40, 47, 74, 88; Saur Bible, 57n17
Blue Laws (Sunday closings), 37, 88
Boston: Catholics in, 60, 61, 75–76n7;
    customs duties paid in, 6; diocese of, 62,
    76n8; Ursuline school for girls in, 67
Boston College, 76n14
Botta, Carlo, xxxn16
Bowditch, Nathaniel, 23, 32n21
Brethren of Moravia, 47
British colonies. *See* English colonies
Brooks, Edward, 79
Brumidi, Constantino, xxviiin7
Burr, Aaron, 17, 31n12

Calvin, John, 34, 44
camp-meetings (Methodists), 41–42
Canada, 2, 59, 63, 72
Canova, Antonio, 23, 31–32n20
Capellano, Antonio, xxviiin7
capital, US, xiii, 30n9
Capitol building: architect of, 76n13;
    description of, 13
Carli, Giovanni Rinaldo, xxix–xxxn16
Carmelites, 91
Carr, Matthew, 63, 76n11
Carroll, John: aspirations for Georgetown,
    x–xi, xiii, xix, xxi, xxiii; death of, xxii,
    61; as first archbishop of Baltimore, 60,
    75n3; as founder of Georgetown, xvi;
    Grassi meeting with (1810), xviii–xix; on
    Grassi's contribution to Georgetown,
    xiii; life of, 60–61
Catherine of Russia, ix
Catholic Church and Catholics, xii, 59–
    78, 82, 90–93; Anglican ordinations
not recognized by, 44, 50; Anglicans
    rejecting tenets of, 43; bequests to,
    70; churches and functions, 67–74;
    contributions to maintain churches, 69;
    conversions, 71–72, 78n23; country church
    services and country folk observing
    proper rituals, 68–69, 71; dioceses in
    America, 62–67; French immigrants and,
    33; Grassi's role in advancing American
    vision for, xiii; infallibility of teachings
    of, 52; last rites, 69; lax observance and
    scandals against religion, 71; Maryland
    as colony of, 10; missionaries, 59, 70, 72;
    prevalence of, 59; religious paintings, 67;
    sacrament of confession as privileged
    information, 36; sick calls, 69; slavery
    and, xxiv–xxv, 70, 72; wine for Holy
    Mass, 4, 51, 90. *See also* anti-Catholicism;
    Dominicans; Jesuits; papism; *specific
    orders, missions, and cities*
Catholick Question in America, 36–37
Causici, Enrico, xxviiin7
celibacy, 47
Charleston, South Carolina: Catholics in,
    61, 64; customs duties paid in, 6
Charleston Schism, xxv
chastity, 38
Cheverus, Jean-Louis Lefebvre de, ix, 50,
    57n21, 62, 76n8
children: customs involving, 17, 85;
    indulgence of, 18, 19; insubordination
    and rebellion of, 19; raising without
    particular religious affiliation, 35. *See also*
    education and literacy
China, Catholic missionaries in, x, xvi–xvii
Chraystians, or Craistians, 47–48, 88
church. *See* Catholic Church and Catholics;
    religion; *specific religious sects*
Church of England. *See* Anglicans
Church of the Brethren (formerly the
    Dunkers), 57n18
Cicero, 21, 86
Cincinnati, Catholics in, 61, 66, 77n16
cities and towns: layout of, 12–13; naming
    of, 15; populations of, 98–99t; vices of city
    dwellers, 17, 84. *See also specific cities*
classes, mixing among, 17, 85

Classical Tour in Italy, The (Eustace), 22,
  31n20
class-meetings (Methodists), 41
Clay, Mrs. Henry, xxii
Clem (enslaved man), xxiv
Clement XIV (pope), xv, 75n5
climate, 2–3
Clinton, Dewitt, 36, 55n3
clothing. *See* dress and appearance
College of Nobles (Belarus), xvi
College of Nobles (Naples), xxv
College of Nobles (Turin), xxv
Columbia: creation of District of, 13; use of
  term, 2
Columbiad (Barlow), 21–22, 31n17, 85
Columbus, Christopher, 2
commerce, xiii, 5–8; import vs. export
  levels, 6; monetary system, 15; number
  of post offices and, 9; weights and
  measures, 15
Conewago mission, 9, 63
Confession of Augsburg, 34
Congregationalists, 35, 39–40, 45, 50, 52,
  78n23, 87, 88
Congress, US: chaplain of, 27, 32n24;
  elections, 25; Georgetown as possible
  meeting place during War of 1812, xxi,
  xxii; Georgetown's ties with, xi; location
  of, 12–13; role of, 25
Connecticut, 38, 98t
Connolly, John, 62, 76n10
Constitution, US: slavery in contrast to,
  xiii, xxiv, 10, 20, 83. *See also specific
  amendments and their topics*
Credo quidquid Catholica credit Ecclesia (I
  believe whatever the Catholic Church
  believes), 69
crime, 14, 35–36, 73–74
Cushing, William, 79
Custis, Eleanor "Nellie" (adopted daughter
  of George Washington), xx
Custis, Mrs. (niece of George Washington),
  xix
customs, 16–19, 84–85

Dallas, Trevanion, xxii
dancing, 17, 46–47, 85

Daughters of Mary at the Foot of the Cross
  (Kentucky), 67, 91
de Andreis, Felix, 66, 77n18
Delaware, 98t
Democracy in America (Tocqueville), xxv–
  xxvi
Democrats, 26
Demosthenes, 21, 86
De Pauw, Cornelius, xxixn16
De Wolf, Countess, 67
Dickens, Charles: *American Notes*, xxvii
discord: among states, 26–27; religious
  discord due to numerosity of sects, 27,
  52, 93
diseases, xiii, 3, 57n21
District of Columbia, 13, 99t
Dominicans, 65, 66, 69, 77n16, 91
dress and appearance, 17, 85
drinking and frequenting taverns, 17, 42,
  84. *See also* wine and alcoholic beverages
Dubois, John, ix, 66, 76n14, 77n21, 91
Dubourg, Louis William Valentine, ix, 65,
  76n15
Duchesne, Philippine, ix
duels, 17–18, 31nn12–13, 85
Dunkers, 47, 57n18, 88
Durkin, J. T., xxviiin8
Dutch Reformed churches, 53

East Indies, 10
economy, 98–99t; agricultural sector, 30n5;
  monetary system and failure of paper
  money, 7–8, 15. *See also* agriculture and
  food; commerce; manufacturing
Edinburgh Review, 20
education and literacy, xiii, 18, 85–86;
  European teachers at boarding
  schools, 19; of girls, 18–19, 66, 77n20,
  85; Lancaster type of school, 18;
  mathematics, 23; rise of public
  education, 31n15; universities or colleges
  by state, 98–99t
Egan, Father (bishop of Philadelphia), xviii
elections, 25, 26
elocution and public speaking, 21, 49, 85–
  86, 89
Emmitsburg, Maryland, 65, 66, 77n16, 91

Endicott, John, 39, 55n7
end-of-world prediction, 38
England: capture of American ships, 7;
    dominance of English character among
    Americans, 15; first American settlers
    from, 8; manufacturing in, 7; referring
    to Americans as Yankees, 16, 84; transfer
    of religious prejudices to America, 37;
    wine in, 4. *See also* English colonies
England, John, ix
English colonies, 8, 10, 39, 43, 60
English language, 15, 20, 70
Enlightenment thinking, xxvi
entertainment, 17. *See also* dancing
Episcopalians. *See* Anglicans
equality, xiii, 26
Erie Canal, 16
Europe: American public character derived
    from, 15; United States compared to, 2,
    12, 14, 17
Eustace, John Chetwode: *The Classical Tour
    in Italy*, 22, 31n20
Evangelical Lutherans, 53

Fayetteville, North Carolina, 64
Federalists, xxxn16, 26
Fenwick, Edward Dominic, 65–66, 77n16
Fesch, Joseph, 68
fine arts and culture, xiii, 22–23; religious
    paintings, 67
Finotti, Giuseppe Maria, xv
fires and firefighting, 14
First Amendment, 33, 55n1
Flaget, Benedict Joseph, ix, 62, 75n6
flag of United States, 26
food. *See* agriculture and food
France: capture of American ships, 7;
    dancing as pastime in, 17, 85; French
    immigrants ceasing to be Catholics,
    33; Jesuits' ill treatment in, xxvi–xxvii;
    opinion of America, 83; republican
    form of government and, 27–28
Franklin, Benjamin, xxxn16
Franzoni, Giuseppe, xix, xx, xxviiin7
Frederick, Maryland, 64, 77n21
Fredericksburg, Virginia, 64

freedom of press, 26, 52
freedom of religion, xiii, 26, 33, 36, 53,
    56n14, 70, 71, 73, 93
freedom of speech, 25, 52
Freeman, James, 45, 56n16
French Revolution, xxvi, 56n15
French settlers: in Kentucky, 63; religion
    of, 33
Friends. *See* Quakers
Fulton, Robert, 24, 32n22
future of United States, xiii, 27–28

Gallitzin, Demetrius Augustine, 63, 76n12
gambling, 17, 84
Gaston, William, xii, xvi, xx, xxi
gazettes, xxiv, 20, 24, 25, 41
Geerts, Father, 67
geography, 3, 98–99t
Georgetown (suburb of Washington):
    Church of the Holy Trinity, 64;
    commerce with, 13; Georgetown
    Visitation Convent, 66, 77n20; militia
    attending various churches in, 35
Georgetown College: academic reputation
    of, xxii; after Grassi's departure, xxvii;
    charter of, xi–xii, xxii; commencement
    exercises as public exhibitions, xi;
    Congress considering as possible
    meeting place during War of 1812,
    xxi, xxii; Corporation of the Roman
    Catholic Clergymen of Maryland in
    charge of, x; Dickens's opinion of, xxvii;
    enslaved persons working at, xxiv;
    faculty of, x–xi; first Catholic degree-
    granting institution in United States,
    xxii; graduates entering seminary, xi;
    Grassi's contribution to, xiii, xv, 32n21;
    Grassi's initial opinion of, x, xix; Grassi's
    initiatives to save, x–xi, xxii–xxiii,
    xxixn13; Indian chiefs visiting, 73; as
    Jesuit institution, xvi, 65, 90; as national
    observatory, xii; recalling Jesuit faculty
    from New York City to, x–xi, xxiii,
    xxixn13, 32n21
Georgia, 99t
German Reformed church, 53

Germans in Philadelphia, 63
Gillespy, Edward, 55n4
Gioberti, Vincenzo, xxvi
government, xiii, 25–26. *See also* republican
    government
Grassi, Giovanni Antonio (John Anthony):
    background in Society of Jesus, ix–x,
    xvi; birth of, xvi; in Chinese mission
    that never reaches China, x, xvi; death
    of, xxvii; diary of, xviii; at Georgetown
    College, x–xi, xviii–xx, 82; health
    problems of, xii, xx, xxv; as Maryland
    Mission superior, x, xx; in Portugal
    seeking passage to China, xvii; return
    to Rome and later positions held in
    Italy, xii, xxii, xxv; in Russia, x, xvi; at
    Stonyhurst College, x, xvii–xviii; in
    United States, ix–xi, xviii, xxviii*n*5;
    US citizenship of, xix, xxii, xxvii,
    xxix*n*11. *See also Notizie varie sullo stato
    presente della repubblica degli Stati Uniti
    dell'America*
Greaton, Joseph, 30n8
greed. *See* wealth, pursuit of
Gruber, Gabriel, xvi

Hamilton, Alexander, 17, 31n12
Harmony Society, 38
Harvard College, 22
Henry IV (king of France), 5, 30n3, 83
Henry, Patrick, xxx*n*16
heresy and heretics, 34, 47, 73, 89, 90
Hill, Father, 66
Historical Review (1819), 7
Holy Trinity, 45, 47
Homer, 21, 85
Hoover, Herbert, 30n3
Horace: *Satires, Epistles, and Ars Poetica*, 20
Houdon, Antoine, 31n21
House of Representatives, US, 25
housing patterns, xiii, 12, 14–15
Hus, John, 57n18

Iardella, Iacopo, xxviii*n*7
Illinois territory, 63, 99*t*
immigrant clergy, role of, ix

Indiana, 99*t*
Indians. *See* American Indians
inheritance laws, 27
insurance industry, 6
Irish settlers in New York state, 62–63
Italian literature, 22
Italians: advice against emigrating to
    America, 12; American views of, 22;
    bequests by, 70; influence on US
    educational system, xv; as stone carvers
    and artists for US Capitol, xix, xx,
    xxviii*n*7; in Washington, xx; as writers
    about North America, xxix*n*16

Jefferson, Thomas, xxviii*n*7, xxix–xxx*n*16,
    31–32n20
Jerusalem Township (New York), 57n19
Jesuits: Georgetown's affiliation with, xvi,
    65, 90; as missionaries to United States,
    xv, 59–60, 62; in New York, 72; under
    papal suppression, ix, x, xv, 60, 73, 75n5,
    91–92; in Philadelphia, 63; reestablished,
    xvi, xxi, 75n5, 91–92
Jews, 38, 53
jury trials, 26

Kentucky, 99*t*; ban on Methodists' camp-
    meetings, 42; Catholic mission in, 77n16,
    77n22; Daughters of Mary at the Foot
    of the Cross in, 67, 91; Dominicans in,
    65, 91; homesteading of, 3; migration of
    Maryland Catholics to, 63
Kilbourne (Kilburn), James, 51, 57n22
Kilgour, Robert, 56n13
Klein-Nicola, Georg, 57n17
Knox, John, 34, 44
Kohlmann, Anthony, xxiii, xxix*n*13, 35–36,
    50, 55nn2–4
Korsack, Father, xvi–xviii

lack of rootedness, xiii, 6
Lafayette, Marquis de, xxx*n*16
Lancaster, Joseph, 31n15
Lancaster, Pennsylvania, 63
land: federal bureau for land sales, 11;
    Maryland land owned by Catholic

land (*continued*)
Church, 70; sale and allotment of, 11.
See also agriculture and food
Latrobe, Benjamin Henry, xxviii*n*7, 64,
76n13
Lee, Henry, xix, xx
Lee, Thomas, xxii
Lee, William, xxii
legal profession, 18
liberality of religion. *See* religion
liberty of conscience, 56n14
libraries, 22
Lima, Kentucky, 65
liquor. *See* wine and alcoholic beverages
Literary Institution (New York), xxiii,
xxix*n*13, 32n21, 65, 90
literature, 19–22; Italian literature
unknown in America, 22
Livingston, Robert R., 32n22
Louis XVIII (king of France), 68
Louisiana, 99*t*
Louisiana Purchase/Territory, 5, 30n4,
77n18
Lowell, John A., 79
Lustyg, Father, xvii
Lutherans, 34, 53, 55n6, 88

Madison, James, xii, xxii, xxix*n*16
Mai, Angelo, xxvii
Maine, 98*t*
Malevè, Francis, 64, 76n14
manners and civility, 17, 84–85
manufacturing, xiii, 5, 7–8, 29–30
Maréchal, Ambrose, ix, 67, 78n24
Marie: Ou l'esclavage aux États-Unis (de
Beaumont), xxvi
Maryland, 98*t*; Catholics in, 10, 60, 64;
Convent of the Discalced Carmelites
of Saint Theresa, 66; Corporation
of the Roman Catholic Clergymen
of Maryland, x, 69–70; Georgetown
College and, xi; migration of Catholics
from, 63
Massachusetts, 38, 98*t*
Mather, Increase, 39, 55n8
Matignon, Francis, 62, 75–76nn7–8
Mazzei, Filippo, xxx*n*16

McElroy, John, xxi, xxvi, xxx–xxxi*n*17,
76n14
medical profession, 18, 21
Methodists, 37, 40–43, 47, 53, 88, 90;
African Methodists, 50, 53; conversion to
Catholicism, 72
Michigan Territory, 99*t*
migration patterns, xiii, 8
Mississippi, 99*t*
Mississippi River, 5
Missouri, homesteading of, 3
Missouri Territory, 99*t*
Mitchill, Dr., 29–30, 82
mixed marriages of Catholics to non-
Catholics, 70–71
mobility. *See* lack of rootedness
monetary system, 7–8, 15, 31n11
Monroe, James, xii, 73
Moore, John Hamilton, 32n21
Moravians, 47, 53
mores and moral order, xiii, 7–8, 22, 27, 42
Mount Saint Mary Seminary of the West,
77n16
Mount Vernon (home of George
Washington), xxi, xxviii*n*9

Napoleonic Wars, 7
Native Americans. *See* American Indians
Nautical Almanac, 23
Navy, US, 23, 25, 26
Neale, Father, xxi
Neale, Francis (Grassi's predecessor at
Georgetown), xxix*n*13, 70
Neale, Leonard (archbishop of Baltimore):
death of, 61; educational initiatives of,
66, 91; as first Catholic bishop ordained
in America, 60, 75n3; Grassi as agent
for, xii, xxv; Maréchal and, 78n24;
welcoming Grassi to Georgetown, xviii
Nerinckx, Charles, 67, 77n22, 91
New Bern, North Carolina, 64
New England: Catholics in, 62; character of
people in, 16, 84; Chraystians/Craistians
in, 47; dominance of Congregationalists
in, 52; most populated region of United
States, 2; public schools in, 18; religion
in, 35, 87; Sabbath travel prohibited in,

37, 88; Yankees, use of term, 16, 84. *See also specific states*

New Hampshire, 98*t*

New Jersey, 98*t*

New Jerusalem (Dunkers sect), 47

New Orleans: Catholics in, 60, 61; customs duties paid in, 6; steamboat traffic and, 5

newspapers, 26

Newton, Thomas, 29

New York (state), 98*t*; Catholics in, 62–63; Quakers in, 46

New York City: banks and insurance companies in, 28; Catholics in, 60, 61; churches (by sect) and religious associations in, 52–53; Church of Saint Patrick, 62, 69; customs duties paid in, 6; diocese of, 62–63, 77n21; firefighting in, 14; scientific establishments and charitable institutions in, 28–29

Norfolk, Virginia: Catholics in, 64; customs duties paid in, 6

North American Review of *Notizie* (1823), 79–93

North Carolina, 99*t*

northern states: agricultural superiority of, 4; inclination to secede, 26; medical students and profession in, 21; piety of and observance of holy days in, 37; slavery abolished in, 4, 10, 84. *See also* New England; *specific states*

North West Territory, 99*t*

Le notizie del giorno (Roman gazette), 25

Notizie varie sullo stato presente della repubblica degli Stati Uniti dell'America settentrionale, scritte al principio del 1818 (Grassi), ix, xii–xiii; Americans should benefit from reading, 86; considered to be a pamphlet, 81; letter sent by Grassi with copy to Georgetown, xxvi; *North American Review* (1823) contemporary book review of, 79–93; publication and editions of, xxv, xxvi, xxviin1; Tocqueville's *Democracy in America* in relation to, xxv–xxvi

novels, publication and popularity of, 16, 22, 84

nuns. *See* women

OAMDG (*Omnia ad majorem Dei gloriam*), 32n25, 74

Ohio, 98*t*; Catholic mission in, 65, 77n16; homesteading of, 3

Ohio River, 5

Omnia ad majorem Dei gloriam (OAMDG), 32n25, 74

Paine, Thomas, 59; *The Age of Reason*, 32n21, 59, 75n1

papism, 43, 44, 52, 53, 92

patents, 24

Paul (saint), 32n21, 38, 42, 46

Peemans, Mr., 67

Pellico, Luigi, xxvi

Pellico, Silvio, xxvi, xxxin18

Penn, William, 10

Pennsylvania, 98*t*; Catholics in, 63; Dunkers in, 47; Harmony Society in, 38; militia, 12–13; Quakers in, 10, 46

Penobscot Indians, 62, 76n9

Petersburg, Virginia, Catholics in, 64

Petrie, Arthur, 56n13

Philadelphia: Catholic orphanage in, 66, 91; Catholics in, 60, 61; customs duties paid in, 6; diocese of, 63; Holy Trinity Church, 63; as previous seat of federal government, 12–13; public library in, 22; as Quaker city, 46; Saint Augustine's, 63; Saint Joseph's, 63; Saint Mary's, 63

Pianciani, Giovanni Battista, xv

Pignatelli, Giuseppe Maria, xvi

Pius VI, 60

Pius VII, xvi, xxi, 75n5

Plymouth, Massachusetts, first settlers in, 39

Poirot, Louis, xvi

political parties, 26

population growth, xiii, 8–15, 30n7, 83, 98–99*t*; compared to Europe, 9; European roots of, 10; number of post offices and, 9; rate of growth, 8–9; treaties as method to acquire lands from American Indians, 10–11

Portsmouth, Virginia, Catholics in, 64
Port Tobacco, Maryland, 66, 77n19, 91
Portugal, xvii, 2
postal service: delivery system, 15–16;
    number of post offices, 9
Potomac River, 2, 3, 13
poverty, 7, 14–15, 18, 71
predestination, 44
Presbyterians, 34, 44, 88. *See also* Puritans
presidency, 26
press, freedom of, 26
pride, 15
Priestley, Joseph, 45, 56n15
Princeton College, 19
Propaganda Fide, xvii
Protestants: European compared to
    American, 49–50, 89; as Georgetown
    students, xi; ministers as term used by,
    70; Walmesley on, 75n4. *See also* anti-
    Catholicism; *specific sects*
public character, xiii, 15–16, 82–83; of
    children, 19
public debt, 6
public speaking. *See* elocution and public
    speaking
public welfare, 18
publishing and printing shops, 21–22
Purgatory, 46
Puritans, 44, 53, 54, 88

quackery, 35
Quakers, 10, 38, 46–47, 88; conversion to
    Catholicism, 71–72

religion, 33–57; awakening period,
    48; baptism, 45, 51, 70, 71; church
    attendance, 35, 87; communion, 45,
    48–49, 51; conversions and switching
    among sects, xiii, 50, 87, 91; criticism
    of religious freedom, 53; critique in
    North American Review of *Notizie*, 86–
    87; discord due to numerosity of sects,
    27, 52, 93; diversity of, 26–27, 33, 50, 87,
    93; excommunication, 49; importance
    of piety, 27, 34, 37, 73, 88; liberality
    of, 34–37, 44, 49, 50, 51, 89; ministers

as Protestant term, 70; ordinations,
    39, 44, 50; preachers, selection of, 47,
    49; preaching, style of, 42, 49, 89;
    principal sects of America, 39–48, 88;
    public prayer, 27; sect, meaning of,
    34; toleration, 93. *See also* freedom of
    religion; separation of church and state;
    specific sects
republican government, 15, 26, 27
Restorationists, Universalists as, 46
resurrection and day of final judgment, 46
Revolution of 1848–49 in Rome, xxvii
Rhode Island, 45, 98*t*
Richmond, Virginia: Catholics in, 61, 64;
    Washington statue in, 22–23, 31–32n20
Ringgold, Mrs. (daughter of Henry Lee),
    xxi
Rosati, Joseph, ix
Rossi, Pellegrino, xxvii, xxxin18
Rush, Benjamin, 21, 31n17
Russia, Jesuits in, ix, xvi

Sabbath observance, 37, 38, 55n5, 88
Salem, Massachusetts, first settlers in, 39
Sampson, William, 55n4
Satires, Epistles, and Ars Poetica (Horace),
    20
Saur Bible, 57n17
Savannah, Georgia: Catholics in, 64;
    customs duties paid in, 6
Saybrook Platform (Congregationalists),
    39, 55–56n9
science. *See* astronomy and science
Scotland, 44, 56n13
Seabury, Samuel, 43–44, 45, 56nn12–13,
    57n20
Secchi, Angelo, xv
secularism, 33, 93
Seminary of Saint Sulpice, 61, 64, 65
Senate, US, xix, xxi, 25
separation of church and state, xiii, 33, 35,
    56n14
Sestini, Benedetto, xv
settlers. *See* English colonies; housing
    patterns; population growth
Severino, Roberto, xiii–xiv

Shakers, 46–47
ship construction and shipbuilding yards, 24–25
Sisters of Charity, 66
Skinner, John, 44, 56n13
slavery and enslaved people, xxiii–xxv, 9–10, 16, 19, 20, 67, 69, 72; abolished in northern states, 4, 10, 84; Catholicism and, xxiv–xxv, 70, 72; as contradiction of US Constitution, xiii, 10, 20, 83; de Beaumont on, xxvi; Georgetown University's sale of enslaved people, xxx–xxxin17; greed of slaveholders, 10, 83–84; marriages not recognized, 70, 78n27; population of enslaved people, 9–10, 83; reasons to perpetuate, 10; religious and superstitious practices of, 10, 84
social customs, 16–19
Society of Jesus. *See* Jesuits
South America, 2
South Carolina, 99t
southern states: agriculture in, 4, 30n5; indulgence of children in, 18; medical students and profession in, 21. *See also* slavery and enslaved people; *specific states*
Southington, Connecticut, 38
Spanish colonies in South America, 10
Spanish piece or dollar, 15, 31n11
speculation, 7–8, 26
speech, freedom of, 25, 52
steam engines and steamships, 5, 16, 24–25, 32n22
Stonyhurst College, x, xvii–xviii
Sulpicians, x, 65, 90
superstitions, 10, 17, 22, 35, 85, 87
Swedenborg, Emanuel, 47, 57n18

technological development, xiii; in agriculture, 4–5; inventions, 24; in manufacturing, 7, 29–30; in sciences, 23
Tennessee, 99t; homesteading of, 3
Thanksgiving, 27
Thayer, John, 67, 78n23, 91
Third Commandment, 37, 88
Tiber Creek, 13, 30n10

tobacco, 4
Tocqueville, Alexis de: *Democracy in America*, xxv–xxvi
trade. *See* commerce
transportation modes, 16. *See also* steam engines and steamships
treaties as method to acquire lands from American Indians, 10–11
trial by jury, 26
Trumbull, John, 23

Unitarians, 45, 56n15, 88
Universalists, 46, 57n17, 88
Ursulines, 67, 91

Vermont, 98t
Vespucci, Amerigo, 2
Vincentians, 77n18, 91
Virgil, 21, 85
Virginia, 98t; anti-Catholicism in, 38; discord with other states, 27; end of world predicted by preacher in, 38
Visitation Order/Visitation Sisters, 66, 77n20, 91

Wabanaki Confederacy, 76n9
Wallace, James, xii, 23, 32n21
Walmesley, Charles (Signor Pastorini), 60, 75n4
Warner, Lord and Lady, 71
War of 1812, xiii, xx–xxii
Washington (capital): climate of, 2; description of, 12–14; Georgetown's role in, xi; Grassi's first impression of, xviii; Grassi's social life in, xx; Library of Congress, 22; longitude of, xii; postal service, 16; Saint Patrick's Church, 64
Washington, George: Carroll and, 61; criticism of, xxxn16; military role of, 31n12; retirement of, 26; selection of national capital's location, 13; statue of, 22–23, 31–32n20
wealth, pursuit of: American characteristic for, 15; commerce and, 6; inheritance and, 27; likelihood of wealthy class to emerge, 27; Quakers and, 46; settlers

wealth, pursuit of (*continued*)
  and migrants, success of the industrious,
  11–12
Weld, Thomas, 60
Wesley, John, 40, 42, 56n10
West, Benjamin, 23
Western states and territories: commerce,
  5; homesteading of, 3; missionaries to,
  66. *See also specific state or territory*
White, Andrew, 60, 75n2
Whitfield, George, 40, 42, 56n10
Wilkinson, Jemima, 48, 57n19
William & Mary College, 19
Williams, Roger, 45, 56n14
Wilson, Alexander: *American Ornithology*,
  21, 31n18

Winchester, Elhanan, 46, 56–57n17
wine and alcoholic beverages, 4, 5, 51,
  83, 90
witchcraft, 38
women: Catholic communities of nuns,
  66–67; as Chraystian/Craistian
  preachers, 47; education of girls, 18–19,
  66, 77n20, 85; as Methodists, 41; Sabbath
  observance by, 88; Wilkinson's role as
  preacher, 57n19
Wycliffe, John, 57n18

Yale College, 50, 57n20
Yankees. *See* New England
yellow fever, 3, 57n21
Young, Nicholas Dominic, 65, 77n16